I0181931

HEAVEN READY WHEN HE CALLS

by Tiffany Atkins

T. D. Atkins Publishing

Copyright © 2012 Tiffany Atkins
All Rights Reserved
ISBN-10: 0983818908
ISBN-13: 9780983818908
Library of Congress Control Number: 2011913729
T. D. Atkins Publishing, Madison, AL

To my loving mother
Her soft tone and encouraging words helped me to hold on

"You can't shake my faith"

A special thank you to the late Bishop G .E. Patterson: a man I never met in person, but whom I deeply admired and respected concerning the things of God. When I was wandering without an earthly shepherd, he unwittingly drew me into the fold as one of his own.

But godliness with contentment is great gain.
For we brought nothing into this world, and it is certain
we can carry nothing out.

1 Timothy 6:6-7

(all scriptures are quoted from the King James Version (KJV)
of the Bible)

INTRODUCTION

When the church as a whole is referenced, different jargon is used to describe it, depending on the context. Sometimes the church as a whole is just referred to as *the Body*, *the Body of Christ*, *the Bride of Christ*, or just as *the Church*. Normally these general terms are used about all churches, without any specific denomination in mind. They are used to describe the body of believers. But the individuals included in these all-encompassing terms have strayed from the very thing that is supposed to define the Church. The Body of Christ has mutated into something that God never intended it to be. Clear instructions are laid out in the Bible on how the Church should behave and how things should be conducted, but we have gotten so far away from the Bible that it has become just a book of suggestions to some, instead of the Word of God.

I was raised in the Church, and I started walking with the Lord at an early age. In less than thirty years on this earth, I have seen the Body disintegrate into what it is today. To say that the Church is a shell of its former self is the biggest understatement of all time. I have grown increasingly aggravated by the current state of the Body of Christ. It is as if the Church has contracted some type of debilitating disease that is causing it to deteriorate from the inside out.

I am in so much pain—mentally, physically, emotionally, and especially spiritually. One of the loves of my life, the Body of Christ, is dying, and I feel helpless to revive it. Diseases have popped up everywhere, and the Body is hemorrhaging. The only way that I can think of to help stop the bleeding is to expose the problems. Hold on, because the covers are coming off. When I hear people talk about twelve-step programs, they often say that the first step is admitting that there is a problem, and then the healing can begin. Well, if that is the case, God, we have a problem!

I am not politically correct, so feelings might get hurt. For anyone about to read this book who is sensitive, I strongly suggest getting girded up before continuing to read. I am not Mary Poppins, and a spoonful of sugar is not going to help this go down any easier. Enough is enough. I have held this in for too long, and it is about to consume me. It's time for me to purge.

To the Disappointed and the Heartbroken —

Get Over It!

When I say "get over it" to the disappointed and the heartbroken, I am not trying to elicit a laugh, nor am I trying to be cruel. But it is a necessary step. I belong in this category myself. I am well aware of the fact that sometimes getting over something is easier said than done. Some disappointments in life can easily be overcome. Then there are those that are not as easy. A situation that involves a casual acquaintance or some unknown person can quickly be overlooked and forgotten, but church hurt and family hurt are two different beasts that are difficult to overcome. Church hurt and family hurt can linger for years, and for some it stays until the day they die. Yet the difficult pain and suffering is imperative to overcome, because they can cause a state of bitterness and depression that are not conducive to a Christian life.

One of the main reasons I see why people are hurt in the Church is because they have placed their faith in man. Jeremiah 17:5, 7, says: *Thus saith the LORD; Cursed be the man that trusteth in man, and maketh flesh his arm, and whose heart departeth from the LORD. Blessed is the man that trusteth in the LORD, and whose hope the LORD is.* The Bible lets us know that when we place our trust in man we are going to have problems, but when we place our

3

faith in God we will be blessed. By *blessed*, the Bible does not mean the pathetic definition of a blessing that we have today. It is referring to a true blessing. When we take our faith away from the Lord and put it in man, in the end there is only one outcome—disappointment. I know the feeling all too well. I have seen people (especially in the Church) whom I love, admire, and respect, fall time and time again, right in front of my eyes. Seeing the same cycle of pastors and ministers of the Gospel falling from grace because of money, sex, power, and other perishable things over and over again caused me to be so heartbroken and disappointed. I can't understand how this has been allowed to go on for so long without an outcry from the people or a revolt by the true pastors and ministers of the Gospel.

Misplaced faith hurts, but most of my disappointment in the Body of Christ has come from the complete and utter disregard for the saved and sanctified in the Church. Saved people are treated as lepers, as if they are an anomaly in the Body. Answer these questions for me:

When did holiness and salvation become bad words in the Church? When did it get to the point that preachers could get up and act like palm readers who will tell anyone they have a blessing on the way as long as they put enough money in the basket? When did we veer so far off course that a pastor gets more people saying "Amen" for quoting something off of the rap and R&B Top 10 than they would get preaching about holiness and salvation? I am saved and I have been since I was a young child. I can say from personal experience that it does not feel good to feel like an organ that the Body has rejected just because I strive to please God and not man. When did preaching holiness and salvation and teaching people how to live right become wrong? I don't know when the pendulum shifted, but it has. Now if someone preaches about living and doing right, they are branded as "self-righteous" instead of being called saved and one of God's chosen. The saved have no place in the Church anymore, and the sad thing is, because of how things are going, God won't have a place in the Church after a while.

Do people even believe anymore? I mean really, church has become nothing more than a business with a high turnover rate. It took me a little while to understand this. When I first came into the knowledge of Christ, I would have to characterize myself as being naive. I thought everybody in church was saved, and they had everyone's best interests at heart. Foolish me. I now understand how people can become bitter in the church building, and I understand how they have to walk away and leave (the church building, not God). People can be sedentary and bitter in the Church because they give their all to the church building, and the building yields nothing in return. These people run around and do things for the church out of the goodness of their hearts. There are times when people neglect their own lives, their families, and other responsibilities, all in the name of helping the church building.

But doing things for the church building (the pastor, his wife, his family, etc.) is like loving someone who doesn't love you back. Loving the church building will always be an unrequited love. The inanimate object will always let you down. Please hear me when I say that there is a difference between loyalty to God and loyalty to the church building and the people in it. The main difference is that God loves us and wants to give us eternal life, but I have seen the church building and the people in it drive others to their grave. People get used like toilet paper, and, once they can no longer perform or provide, they are disposed of. There are people in the Church who are torn because they are not able to separate the church building from the Church that the Lord will call up to meet Him. I have seen men and women devote their lives (literally) to the church building. Not to God, but to the building. Every time the church doors open, they were there. Now they look up and are in their late thirties, forties, and sometimes fifties, and it seems as if life has passed them by.

Where are the people in the Church who have no problem telling the women, "Yes, I know that we have four services on Sunday, countless during the week, and conferences, etc., but you better pick one, maybe two, and then go home and spend some time with your husband so his eyes won't start wandering"? Where are the people who will tell the men to go home and spend some time with their wives so that they won't long for the touch of a man and go get it somewhere else? Where are the people who will tell the parents to go home and spend some time with their children, so their children won't grow up and resent the Lord because of how their parents cherished the church building more than they cherished their own children?

I hope that I am not being misunderstood. I know that Hebrews 10:25 states that we are not to forsake the assembly of ourselves with one another, but at the same time I also know that people should not be reduced to ashes, and families should not be torn apart, because of the church building. Understand that God is not divisive. People may be, but God is not. In the midst of doing the work for the church building, some have taken their eyes off of the original reason that they became a Christian and started working in the church in the first place.

I am going to impart a little knowledge that most pastors, deacons, or whoever runs the church building will never say. If someone misses a night of the revival to go watch their child play in a basketball game, they are not going to hell. If someone misses a night of church or Sunday morning service because it is their spouse's birthday, they are not going to hell. Contrary to popular belief, it is quite possible to show the love of God outside of the church building. We are to love God and devote ourselves to Him; don't let the church building become a false idol. Good works in the church building cannot save anyone. That building will not love anyone back—I don't care how much people want it to. *The horseleach hath two daughters, crying, Give, give. There are three things that are never satisfied, yea, four things say not, It is enough* (Proverbs 30:15). The parasites and leeches in the church building are never satisfied. They will just find another host after they have destroyed the one that they are currently bleeding dry of money, time, and sanity.

For the disappointed and the heartbroken, hold fast in the Lord. Here is my tough love to the disappointed and the heartbroken—get over it. Now be honest. How many people thought that they were going to skate through life and have no problems? How many people consider themselves to be higher than the Lord himself? How can we think that we are going to have a trouble-free life while the King of kings and the Lord of lords had to endure hell on earth? Since Jesus had to endure persecution from the Pharisees and the Sadducees, and rejection from His own (John 1:11), what makes us think that we are going to have it any different?

The pain of church hurt is unbearable at times. It is as if I would welcome physical pain to take my mind off everything else. But I had to own up to my responsibility in the hurt and pain that I have experienced. I took my eyes off God and placed them on someone who could not live up to my expectations. I placed my hope and faith in one of the creations instead of placing it on the Creator. I tried to make people who were not God fill His shoes. Needless to say, they could not. So a good portion of my hurt and pain is no one's fault but my own. I mentioned that the Body of Christ is one of the loves of my soul. I have learned that this love can bring enormous amounts of joy and also cause me excruciating pain.

> *Therefore to him that knoweth to do good, and doeth it not, to him it is sin.*

> James 4:17

SIDE BAR: FAMILY

Is Blood Really Thicker Than Water?

Church hurt and family hurt: What can I say about family hurt? What can I say about my family, my relatives, and our trials and tribulations? Whoever said misery loves company has apparently never met some of my relatives. If they were to meet my relatives they would come to the same conclusion that I have. Misery doesn't want company. What misery wants is a companion. Company comes and goes, but a true companion stays to the bitter end. As long as some of my relatives are miserable, they want others to be miserable, too. God forbid anyone around them should even resemble being happy. Being happy and satisfied would probably make them internally combust. The sad thing is that they bring the misery on themselves, but they always manage to make their circumstances someone else's fault. I am in utter amazement at times when the relatives who cause ninety-five percent of the family problems have the nerve to complain that the family has problems! As if they have nothing to do with it! It is as if some of my relatives would no longer be able to function if they could not wreak havoc on others. I guess they get the same high causing a fight that most addicts get when they indulge in their addiction. I guess being addicted to misery is like any other addiction; the longer the person has it the more of a tolerance they build up for it. They now have to cause more damage to get the same high. I have more compassion toward addicts who are addicted to some type of substance than those addicted to misery. At least those addicted to substance have somewhat of an excuse for their behavior (in my mind at least).

Some of my relatives can't seem to do anything but cause chaos and confusion, and they have decided that this is what they are going to leave to the next generation. I cringe when I think about how some of my relatives have tried to pass down animosity and wickedness to the next generation as if it were an inheritance to be proud of. They will fall out of love (or what they have distorted love to be) over envy, jealousy, pure hatred, a few hundred dollars, a couch, and a dresser. Really? Does family mean that little to people now? Really? I must have been asleep or dozed off a little bit. When did we put a price tag on love and family? How do people plan to explain their behavior to God? How can someone possibly tell God on the Day of Judgment that they expect to get into heaven after the way that they have treated their own family? They would prefer to die and go to hell than to say "I'm sorry" and let the family heal. There is no accountability anymore. It is always someone else's fault. No one takes responsibility for their actions anymore. Everyone is too proud to apologize, but always thinks that someone should apologize to them. If we are not careful, this haughtiness will engulf the next generation, and we may get to a point that only God can mend the family relationship. The saddest thing of all is that when we do wrong to one another, we know it, but we are too proud to admit that we are wrong. Think about it. Is pride and being hateful worth an eternity in hell? We can quote the Bible like nobody's business, but can't seem to live it. I have a suggestion. Read the Bible and live it; then you have the right to quote it to others.

Wrath is cruel, and anger is outrageous; but who is able to stand before envy?

Proverbs 27:4

A new commandment I give unto you, That ye love one another; as I have loved you, that ye also love one another. By this shall all men know that ye are my disciples, if ye have love one to another.

John 13:34–35

Put on therefore, as the elect of God, holy and beloved, bowels of mercies, kindness, humbleness of mind, meekness, longsuffering;
Forbearing one another, and forgiving one another, if any man have a quarrel against any: even as Christ forgave you, so also do ye.

Colossians 3:12–13

For where envying and strife is, there is confusion and every evil work.

James 3:16

He that loveth his brother abideth in the light, and there is none occasion of stumbling in him.

1 John 2:10

11

My little children, let us not love in word, neither in
tongue; but in deed and in truth.

1 John 3:18

Beloved, let us love one another: for love is of God; and
every one that loveth is born of God, and knoweth God.
He that loveth not knoweth not God; for God is love.
Beloved, if God so loved us, we ought also to love one
another.
No man hath seen God at any time. If we love one another,
God dwelleth in us, and his love is perfected in us.
And we have known and believed the love that God hath
to us.
God is love; and he that dwelleth in love dwelleth in God,
and God in him.

1 John 4:7–8, 11–12, 16

The issues of family and love have weighed on my heart for a long
time. I normally pretend I don't see things to keep the peace, but
no more. People have been doing wrong for so long, and no one
has called them out or corrected them, so they think that their
wrong is right. For a long time I found it easier to love total
strangers than to even like my own relatives. I guess it is because
a total stranger has never hurt me the way that my relatives have.
They seem to purposely make it difficult to even want to be in the
same room with them or to call them to see how they are doing.
I sit back sometimes and try to see when things got this bad. The
sad part about it is so much of this started before I was even born,
and these situations have still not been rectified. How sad is that?

It's really sad to me. Especially since a large portion of my family claims to be Christians. If we are Christians, how then can we not come together in love, resolve our issues, and restore our family? Pride is not at stake here. Generations are on the line. The current and future generations should be more important than anybody's personal demons that they feel the need to inflict on others.

From what I have observed, family will see your children doing wrong and doing things behind your back, and instead of correcting your children, they encourage the wrong and try to hide it from you. Some people have a seriously misguided sense of adulthood. They seem to think that rebellion, if not initiated early on by the child, should be encouraged as a sort of rite of passage like the chicken pox. When I was little, if a child didn't have the chicken pox by a certain age, then that child was placed near a child with the chicken pox so that the uninfected child could go ahead and contract it. That seems to be what is going on in families lately. If children are not rebellious after a certain period of time, then grown folks (inside and outside of the family) actually try to induce rebellion (misery is trying to find a companion again). Just because their kids turned on them, they try to cause division in other people's homes. The Bible says:

Thou shalt not see thy brother's ox or his sheep go astray, and hide thyself from them: thou shalt in any case bring them again unto thy brother.
And if thy brother be not nigh unto thee, or if thou know him not, then thou shalt bring it unto thine own house, and it shall be with thee until thy brother seek after it, and thou shalt restore it to him again.
In like manner shalt thou do with his ass; and so shalt thou do with his raiment; and with all lost thing of thy

*brother's, which he hath lost, and thou hast found, shalt
thou do likewise: thou mayest not hide thyself.
Thou shalt not see thy brother's ass or his ox fall down by
the way, and hide thyself from them: thou shalt surely help
him to lift them up again.*

Deuteronomy 22:1–4

What kind of relative tells young men not to listen to their mother, to stop calling her, to not be a "Mama's boy" just because that young man loves his mother? What kind of a relative tells young ladies to turn away from their mother, and all the while that relative is trying to seep in and cause confusion in the home? If some young men and women would not be so quick to be grown, and stop and listen, they could avoid a lot of unnecessary trouble in their lives. Deuteronomy 22:1–4 means that we are not to stand by and allow our brother or sister's family to run amuck if we can help it. We are definitely not to encourage strife in our brother's or sister's home. We are not to revel in other's misery, but try to help them. If something is going awry in my brother's or sister's house, I should not enjoy it, nor should I act like I don't see it. The Bible lets me know that I have a duty to my brother, my sister, and my God to try to help as best I can to make my family whole again.

I can't speak for my brothers and sisters, but I can speak for me. My mother risks our friendship and me being angry with her by telling me things about life. But she does not withhold the chastening that I need so that she can stay in my good graces. I love the fact that my mother loves me enough to point out the potholes on the road of life, instead of sitting back and watching me fall on my face. I have been able to avoid many problems in life because of what other people would consider "interference" on her part. The way I see it, I have nothing of such monumental proportions going on that I cannot talk with my mother. No matter how old I get, I will still be my mother's child. I don't understand caving under peer pressure. If people can't take being mocked for being a good child, being called "Goody Two-shoes," or a "Mama's boy," or something of that nature, then how will they stand up to the constant ridicule of being a Christian? I would prefer to be John, the disciple whom Jesus loved (John 20:2), and follow Christ amid the laughter and scorn than to be Peter and deny Him. I won't deny my mother the same way I won't deny my Lord and Savior. If I deny my mother, I am shortening my days (Ephesians 6:1–3), and if I deny Christ before man, He will deny me before His Father (Matthew 10:33).

Whatever happened to families staying together? Because in the end, family is all we have. I love my family. I love all of my relatives, but sometimes I don't understand the things that they do, especially when these things are done under the banner of Christianity, as if God were pleased.

That no man go beyond and defraud his brother in any matter: because that the Lord is the avenger of all such, as we also have forewarned you and testified.
1 Thessalonians 4:6

To the Babies in Christ—

Grow Up!

The word *babies* should not be taken in the context of age alone. When I say "babies," I am not referring to newborns out of their mothers' wombs, but to those who are new to Christ. There are some older people who are just now coming into the knowledge of God as well. There are some fifty- and sixty-year-old babies out there. I don't mean "grow up" in a bad way, but babies in Christ are impressionable, vulnerable, and easily manipulated. There are basic things that babies in Christ need to know: don't get caught up with the people and cliques in the church, don't fall for any- and everything, and know the God you serve for yourself. Babies in Christ are similar to regular babies. They emulate what they see. So if a baby in Christ goes to a lukewarm church, it is almost certain that that baby will grow to be a lukewarm Christian. Lukewarm Christian is an oxymoron, because in Revelation 3:15–16 the Lord says, *I know thy works, that thou art neither cold nor hot: I would thou wert cold or hot. So then because thou art luke-warm, and neither cold nor hot, I will spue thee out of my mouth.* To the babies, being lukewarm is a definite way to get a one-way bus ticket to hell on the Day of Judgment, and there are no refunds or substitutions.

The quickest way for a baby to drown in the Body is to try to join the cliques in the church building. Some people actually think that these groups of people are saved, and that the group could teach them how to live right and walk with the Lord. The cliques were formed before you got there, and they will still be there after you leave. I have seen people try to break into these family cliques, or these cliques of people who have been friends for decades. The same thing happens each time. The new person gets taken advantage of and then cast aside. Life still goes on for everyone else, except for that person who was used and abused, because they are so disheartened at that point. They thought that they had a "second family." Now they have to find a way to continue to walk with God and get over their devastation. Wake up. Stop trusting everybody in the church building. Think about it. I was not saved the first time I walked in a church. So it would be foolish of me to assume that everyone else in the church building is saved as well. Salvation is not obtained based on time in church. It doesn't matter if someone was literally birthed in the pews and has been in the church building for thirty years; that doesn't mean that they are saved and have a relationship with the Lord.

Not every one that saith unto me, Lord, Lord, shall enter into the kingdom of heaven; but he that doeth the will of my Father which is in heaven.
Many will say to me in that day, Lord, Lord, have we not prophesied in thy name? and in thy name have cast out devils? and in thy name done many wonderful works?
And then will I profess unto them, I never knew you: depart from me, ye that work iniquity.

Matthew 7:21–23

Some things are easily faked on the surface. Not everyone who has the outward appearance of spiritual gifts (1 Corinthians 12:1–31) is saved. People with certain talents are not saved. Speaking in tongues and shouting are some of the most mimicked spiritual gifts and praise. The Scripture lets us know that not everybody who has the outward appearance of holiness is going to make it into heaven. When I was younger, there was a saying that we had in the church: "God don't need no matches; He's fire all by Himself." That basically means that you don't have to fake holiness to help God out. God's got it. He doesn't need any help from us; we need help from Him. Do not follow man. I can quote bishops and some televangelists all day long, but they are not my God. If they were to fall from grace, I would not fall with them, because I don't worship and praise them. I worship and praise God. If they fall from grace, I will pray for them, keep my eyes on God, and my hand in the Master's hand.

In Acts, Paul speaks to a group of people.

(For all the Athenians and strangers which were there
spent their time in nothing else, but either to tell, or to hear
some new thing.)
Then Paul stood in the midst of Mars' hill, and said,
Ye men of Athens, I perceive that in all things ye are too
superstitious.
For as I passed by, and beheld your devotions, I found
an altar with this inscription, TO THE UNKNOWN
GOD. Whom therefore ye ignorantly worship, him declare
I unto you.
God that made the world and all things therein, seeing
that he is Lord of heaven and earth, dwelleth not in tem-
ples made with hands;

19

*Neither is worshipped with men's hands, as though he
needed any thing, seeing he giveth to all life, and breath,
and all things;*

*And hath made of one blood all nations of men for to dwell
on all the face of the earth, and hath determined the times
before appointed, and the bounds of their habitation;*

*That they should seek the Lord, if haply they might feel
after him, and find him, though he be not far from every
one of us:*

*For in him we live, and move, and have our being; as
certain also of your own poets have said, For we are also
his offspring.*

*Forasmuch then as we are the offspring of God, we ought
not to think that the Godhead is like unto gold, or silver,
or stone, graven by art and man's device.*

Acts 17:21–29

These people Paul spoke to were, for lack of a better term, wishy-washy "believers" who didn't know what they believed. They were in worship, but did not understand or know who or what they were worshipping. That is how some of the babies in Christ are. One minute they are worshipping God, and over time they begin to worship their pastor or other people in the church building. They have fallen into an infinite loop. Eventually they are worshipping because that is what people do on Sunday, but they don't know in whom they believe or why they worship. God should not be unknown to us, nor should we be in constant search of something new (Acts 17: 21). It is okay to want to read the Bible and pray so that we can learn all facets of God, but it is not okay to have a different god or idol every week. Sometimes new believers are like that, and that state of mind is very dangerous. This makes a person double minded. The Bible informs us: *A double minded man is unstable in all his ways* (James 1:8). A double-minded person has no roots and will sway any way the wind blows. God is the same yesterday, today, and forever. Don't make the mistake of trying to continually find something new. There is nothing new under the sun (Ecclesiastes 1:9). God is the same, but He will reveal Himself little by little to those who read His Word and diligently seek Him. Jumping from one doctrine to another shows a lack of knowledge of God, like a flashing neon light. It also makes you ripe for the picking whether it is from the occult, an unscrupulous pastor, or any number of people.

Babies in Christ should recognize the fact that they are babies in Christ. There seems to be a bad connotation with the word *baby*, so people try to act more grown up then they actually are. This is a very dangerous thing to do when walking under the banner of Christianity. Babies need to know that they are babies, so that they don't try to take on things that they don't understand and cannot handle.

Then certain of the vagabond Jews, exorcists, took upon them to call over them which had evil spirits the name of the LORD Jesus, saying, We adjure you by Jesus whom Paul preacheth.
And there were seven sons of one Sceva, a Jew, and chief of the priests, which did so.
And the evil spirit answered and said, Jesus I know, and Paul I know; but who are ye?
And the man in whom the evil spirit was leaped on them, and overcame them, and prevailed against them, so that they fled out of that house naked and wounded.

*And this was known to all the Jews and Greeks also
dwelling at Ephesus; and fear fell on them all, and the
name of the Lord Jesus was magnified.*

Acts 19:13–17

There is nothing wrong with being a baby in Christ, but
it is imperative that the growing process commence rapidly.
Demons can overwhelm if one perceives himself to be bigger than
he actually is. Don't try to handle demons, or anything else for
that matter, if the Lord has not truly prepared you. Evil spirits
will prevail if we try to rise up against them without any power.
At the time a person accepts Jesus Christ as their Lord and Savior,
that person is not yet ready to handle the demons in this world.
The Holy Spirit shields us and protects us while we grow in God
and receive power to fight off the devil and his army. If young
Christians began to get too big for their britches and think that
they can handle the devil based on what they have seen and heard
instead of on their level and relationship with the Lord, then it is
highly probable that the devil will prevail. Strive to grow in God,
but at the same time use wisdom and know where you actually
are spiritually, so that you don't put yourself in a position where
the devil can overtake you.

Babies, please don't be disheartened by what the eyes see. I
understand that people in the church building with true holiness
are ostracized, and those with a form of godliness are praised.
Babies, please be mindful that this may be how people get by
down here, but God is not pleased. No matter what is seen and
what is heard, it is impossible to live contrary to the Word of
God, and still be saved and be a Christian. Some people are under
the impression that once saved always saved. That is not so. It is

quite possible to backslide. Yes, the Lord is married to the back-slider (Jeremiah 3:14), but if the backslider does not renew his vows he will lift up his eyes in hell with the rest of the sinners.

The Bible is filled with people who had God's hand on them and lost their anointing and God's favor because of their actions. The priest Eli allowed his unruly and ungodly sons to do whatever they wanted to do in God's house and to God's people. Not only did God remove Eli's sons, but He removed Eli as well for allowing their bad behavior to go on (1 Samuel 2:12–36; 1 Samuel 4:18). Saul is another example. Saul was anointed to be king of Israel (1 Samuel 10:1–13), but because of his disobedience he was rejected by God (1 Samuel 13:1–14). Eli was a priest and a judge for forty years, and God replaced him with Samuel because of what Eli allowed to take place in the Lord's house. Saul was anointed to be king for a short period of time before he fell from grace in God's eyes, and then David was anointed. No matter how long we have been in the Church, we can be replaced if we fall out of the will of God. Each time God needed to replace someone, their replacement was already in position so the will of God would not suffer. Samuel and David were born to carry the mantle that their predecessors dropped and discarded.

In the Bible Eli and his sons, and Saul and most of his descendents, were killed off. Today when God shifts people around who stray from His will, because they are of the mind-set "once saved always saved", He may not physically kill off the individuals, but they are dead in spirit. So, once saved and sanctified does not mean that we will be like that forever. We have to stay in the will of God. The Bible says, *We know that whosoever is born of God sinneth not; but he that is begotten of God keepeth himself, and that wicked one toucheth him not* (1 John 5:18). This passage does not mean that once a person is saved that they can never sin again. And this passage should not be used as a "license to sin." What the Bible is saying is that when we are saved, we are born of God. If we are never saved or in a backslidden state, then we are not born of God, and we cannot apply this Scripture to ourselves. We are made in the image of God (Genesis 1:26), yes. Does being made in God's image guarantee us a place in heaven, no. No man can pluck us out of God's hand (John 10:25-30), but we can walk away from God ourselves. We can cause ourselves to be disinherited, and we become illegitimate. An illegitimate child will not inherit from the Father. The ultimate inheritance from our heavenly Father is eternal life. When we sin, we fall out of the will of God. People who at one time claimed the name of Christ but didn't do so "unto death" will not make it into heaven. *Fear none of those things which thou shalt suffer: behold, the devil shall cast some of you into prison, that ye may be tried; and ye shall have tribulation ten days: be thou faithful unto death, and I will give thee a crown of life* (Revelation 2:10). We are not guaranteed a place in heaven just because we say we believe, if we don't live right and stay saved until the breath of life leaves our bodies. Life is not jail, and a favorable sentence of eternity in heaven is not negotiable when we stand before the Lord on the Day of Judgment. We have to be faithful unto death. We will not receive credit for time served and be allowed to stop being faithful early.

Get off the breast milk and get some meat.

For when for the time ye ought to be teachers, ye have need that one teach you again which be the first principles of the oracles of God; and are become such as have need of milk, and not of strong meat.
For every one that useth milk is unskilful in the word of righteousness: for he is a babe.

But strong meat belongeth to them that are of full age,
even those who by reason of use have their senses exercised to
discern both good and evil.

Hebrews 5:12–14

It is imperative that all Christians and newcomers to Christ know the Lord for themselves. A sure sign of infancy is for a person to take someone's word for the things of God (the breast milk). Read the Bible and develop a personal relationship with the Lord (the meat). Here is some advice that I was given as a child: read the book of Proverbs. There are thirty-one chapters in the book of Proverbs, and no month has more than thirty-one days. Every day, read a chapter of Proverbs that corresponds with the day of the month. It will help with everyday living, but remember it is not to replace other reading of the Scriptures.

If you are just now starting to read your Bible, in conjunction with reading Proverbs, start reading the Gospels (Matthew, Mark, Luke, and John) and work through the Bible, reading and meditating on the Word of God. The Gospels are the basis of Christianity. They tell of the life, death, burial, and resurrection of Christ. Contrary to what some people think, they don't contradict each other. They are merely written from different perspectives. If four people today were to give an account of the same event that took place, there would be four versions of the event—not that some were lying and some were telling the truth, but it was told from different points of view. Some may dwell on one instance, while others would briefly mention it and dwell on other aspects of the event. That is how the Gospels were written. That does not mean that the Gospels do not overlap, because they do, but each book has a different purpose and a different perspective. But all Scripture is given by inspiration of God (2 Timothy 3:16).

There are standards that the Lord has for His people. The Bible tells us to use wisdom; it does not tell us to be foolish. Believe in God, not these pastors. Remember, there is nothing pure in this world. If people see a way to swindle others, chances are they are going to take it. But my faith is in God, not man. If my faith was in man, every time he wavered, I would, too. When a personal relationship with the Lord is established, then the babies will no longer be babies and they will be able *to discern both good and evil* (Hebrews 5:14). Know the Lord for yourself. Like He knew Jeremiah, God knew us before we were in our mother's womb (Jeremiah 1:5). The least we could do is take the time to pray and study the Bible to know our God.

When I was a child, I spake as a child, I understood as a child, I thought as a child: but when I became a man, I put away childish things.

1 Corinthians 13:11

To the Single Men and Women —

Keep Your Eyes Open and Your Legs Closed!

Single men and women are inconsistent creatures. People have a tendency to stereotype them, but it is very difficult to place them all in one basket. At times single people seem to want to get married, almost to the point of desperation, and then there are times when single people want to "play house" and stay single for as long as possible, so they can be "free." Being desperate and playing house, while not the only issues concerning single people, are the traits that I have seen the most, and they are very detrimental to one's walk with God.

Desperation in any context makes people do things that they would not normally do. It is a very bad state to be in. Desperation causes a clouding of the senses and the spirit. Desperation will cause a good man or woman to abandon all that they know to be true to get what they think they need to survive. For example, women sometimes feel the need to be married by a certain date or a certain age. When that date or that age comes and goes, then that singular event plunges many women into a desperate state. They have now branded themselves as spinsters, or worse, they now feel bad and/or embarrassed because no one has chosen them. Sometimes family, friends, and society don't

27

make things any easier. Some women get married at nineteen, and some get married at thirty-nine. The woman who gets married at thirty-nine should not be made to feel like a leper for those twenty years until the day that she says "I do."

That is how it should be, but that is not the way that it is. Women are constantly being made to feel less than valuable because they are not with somebody. Now that the woman is in a desperate state and to stimulate the marriage process, she will now accept anything. Ladies, please don't settle for five years' worth of happiness just to say you have someone, only to endure a lifetime of hell. Wait on the Lord. I have seen so many unequally yoked couples, inside and outside of the Church. There are people who didn't wait on the Lord, and they are still paying for the decision that they made. I don't care how they try to make it seem on the outside, either the wife is sweet as she can be and the husband is a ho bag, or the husband is in line with God and the wife is a witch. There are saved women who have unsaved husbands, and there are saved men who have to deal with unsaved wives. If asked, I believe that the unequally yoked saved men and women who are married would tell the single folks to wait on the Lord. The pain for not waiting is not worth it.

> *Be ye not unequally yoked together with unbelievers: for*
> *what fellowship hath righteousness with unrighteousness?*
> *and what communion hath light with darkness?*
> *And what concord hath Christ with Belial? or what part*
> *hath he that believeth with an infidel?*
> *And what agreement hath the temple of God with idols?*
> *for ye are the temple of the living God; as God hath said, I*
> *will dwell in them, and walk in them; and I will be their*
> *God, and they shall be my people.*

Wherefore come out from among them, and be ye separate, saith the Lord, and touch not the unclean thing; and I will receive you.

2 Corinthians 6:14–17

Single men and women, please learn how to stand strong and wait on the Lord. Depression coupled with real or perceived ridicule is why some grab the first thing they see and settle. Don't try to be happy for the moment at the risk of being miserable later, just for the sake of having someone.

Lines become blurred under the cloud of desperation. People begin to mutate Scripture to defend their actions. People begin naming and claiming other people's husbands and wives, even in the Church. The Bible says in 1 Corinthians 7:2, *Nevertheless, to avoid fornication, let every man have his own wife, and let every woman have her own husband.* The Bible says get your own. Stop naming and claiming other folks' stuff. If I want a certain type of car, I don't go steal my neighbor's. I go to the dealership and buy one. There is more than one car out there, just like there is more than one man or woman out there.

Now granted, finding a suitable mate isn't as easy as going to buy a car, but being with someone else's husband or wife is committing at least three sins at one time: fornication, adultery, and theft. Since sin is sin, then theft is theft. Just like I am not permitted to steal someone's car, God is not going to let it pass if I steal another woman's husband either. This applies to the men, too. Men can't go steal another man's wife. I don't care if these people are saying that their marriages are "basically over." Yes, the Bible does say, ask and it shall be given unto you (Matthew 7:7), but we cannot get what we ask for sometimes, because we are asking amiss. James 4:3 says, *Ye ask, and receive not, because ye ask amiss, that ye may consume it upon your lusts.* Stop to think about the reasons behind asking God for something. I sincerely doubt that God is going to bump someone to the top of the list for a mate just because they are horny and can't control themselves any longer.

I have never understood playing house instead of getting married. Most women have been planning their weddings since they were young girls. I am sometimes in awe as I watch these silver-tongued men con these women into believing that marriage is just a piece of paper, and because they are in love marriage is not necessary. I remember hearing the late Bishop G. E. Patterson say, "You ought to make a man at least treat you better than he treats his dog because he has to have papers for his dog." I constantly wonder where these ladies' self-esteem is. Do they think so little of themselves that they don't feel as if they are worth more than a dog? If anyone is playing house then it is fornication, period. Fornicating is a sin. All these young men have to do is tell the ladies that they love them and they get what they want (this goes the other way around too—women are cunning as well).

Jeremiah 17:9 says, *The heart is deceitful above all things, and desperately wicked: who can know it?* The heart can get people in so much trouble. I have observed that men and women seem to flock to people that they are trying to "fix." Without God, there is no turning a ho into a housewife, and no turning a pimp into a provider (I had to throw that last part in because of the double standard—people seem to be quick to belittle women, but they make excuses for men because "boys will be boys"). Stop trying to change people. Only God can change someone. Stop clinging to someone, thinking that if they are around you long enough that they will change. A change is going to happen, but they may end up changing you instead of you changing them, or you might just "fix" them and they leave you and become a good husband or good wife for someone else.

Nobody denies themselves anymore. Young, old, married, single, it doesn't matter. Today people see something, they want it, and they try to get it. Sometimes we don't care if it is someone else's. The really good shysters will try to use Scripture like Psalm 84:11, *For the LORD God is a sun and shield: the LORD will give grace and glory: no good thing will he withhold from them that walk uprightly,* to try to justify their sin. No, God won't withhold any good thing from those who walk upright before Him, but if people are trying to get somebody else's stuff they are not walking upright, so they shouldn't expect to get what they asked for.

I think that people should learn to be happy on their own before they find a companion. The reason I say this is because if a man or a woman meets someone who they claim "completes them," and that person left, whether they died or walked out, where does that leave the individual? Are they no longer "completed"? Do they now feel less than or inadequate? Be whole and be happy with yourself and God, because if happiness is hinged on another person it is just as fleeting as that person is, and happiness can elude you as a person can. God knows that it is not good for man to be alone (Genesis 2:18), so until He sends someone, be happy and content.

> *Marriage is honourable in all, and the bed undefiled: but whoremongers and adulterers God will judge.*
>
> Hebrews 13:4

To the Married Men and Women—

Follow Instructions!

I sincerely hope that when the Bridegroom comes back for His bride, His marriage is not like some of the ones that I have seen. Love, honor, and respect have been exchanged with resentment, hatred, and envy. Proverbs 18:22 says, *Whoso findeth a wife findeth a good thing, and obtaineth favour of the LORD.* Apparently, some men have become like Adam. They accept the favor, but will pass the blame on to God for all of their shortcomings, because of the woman that He gave them (Genesis 3:12). Now notice men... this Scripture says "findeth a wife," not whoever finds a baby mama or a quickie at the club. If you were truly searching for a wife and not a quickie, you would have taken the time to know if she was truly a good thing and a gift from God. Years ago I heard someone say that "if you can buy her then she ain't the one." And that is so true, because just like salvation, a gift from the King is free. They have to be given, they can't be stolen or bought. So if buying affection is necessary, then I strongly suggest keeping the receipt and taking it back.

Marriage shouldn't be a fallback plan. These young people are shacking up and living in sin, and no one is saying anything about it. The preachers are not preaching against it, so they think that what they are doing is all right. Holiness, salvation, and keeping yourselves until marriage isn't taught anymore. It seems that the message in the Church now is have a baby, and then get married later. That is the only time marriage seems to come up, when the young lady gets pregnant. Now embarrassment sets in, and everybody is scrambling to get the young lady married off. People are so quick to try to marry off these babies who are living in sin that no one bothers to tell them that a ring isn't enough to get back in right standing with God. True repentance is necessary to wipe the slate clean. That ring on their finger may be a cloak so that others can't see, but God sees. If repentance doesn't come with that ring, then they are still in error. Time may heal all wounds, but time doing right does not negate the time that was used doing wrong. Only repentance can wipe away the wrong.

I see things inside and outside of the Church. When I see these insecure men that belittle their wives in the Church, and then the men try to get up and preach, it kills me. There are few things that are worse than a man being present in the body and absent in the spirit. I really want to walk up to these guys and ask them, "Why are you constantly fighting with the gift that God gave you?" I have seen so many men in the Church (notice how I am refraining from using the term "men of God") who are just boiling over with envy and contempt for their wives.

Husbands, love your wives, even as Christ also loved the church, and gave himself for it;
That he might sanctify and cleanse it with the washing of water by the word,
That he might present it to himself a glorious church, not having spot, or wrinkle, or any such thing; but that it should be holy and without blemish.

34

So ought men to love their wives as their own bodies. He
that loveth his wife loveth himself.
For no man ever yet hated his own flesh; but nourisheth
and cherisheth it, even as the Lord the church:
For we are members of his body, of his flesh, and of his
bones.

Ephesians 5:25–30

Husbands, love your wives, even as Christ also loved the church,
and gave himself for it. I thought that Ephesians 5:25 deserved to
be repeated. I have not finished reading the Bible in its entirety,
but even so, I don't recall any domestic violence calls against
my Lord and Savior because dinner was not ready promptly
at six. I'm also fairly certain that the Bridegroom went off to
prepare a place for His bride (John 14:1–3), and He is not off
shacking up with another woman. Since husbands are to love
their wives as their own flesh, maybe some husbands should
try beating themselves and throwing themselves down a flight
of stairs before they do it to their wives. Then they would see
how uncomfortable it is, and they would know that it doesn't
feel too good, so maybe they wouldn't do it to their wives. The
Word of God lets us know, *No man ever yet hated his own flesh; but*
nourisheth and cherisheth it, even as the Lord the church (verse 29). So
since husbands are to treat their wives as their own flesh, then
they should not do anything to their wives that they would not
like done to them. (Remind anyone of something? The Golden
Rule perhaps [Matthew 7:12]?). From now on, men, especially
men in the Church, try thinking about the Christian way to
handle a family situation.

Women, be in subjection to your husbands. I'm not going to lie. That phrase does not exactly roll off the tongue for me, but according to the Scripture it has to be done.

> *Likewise, ye wives, be in subjection to your own husbands;*
> *that, if any obey not the word, they also may without the*
> *word be won by the conversation of the wives;*
> *While they behold your chaste conversation coupled with*
> *fear.*
> *Whose adorning let it not be that outward adorning of*
> *plaiting the hair, and of wearing of gold, or of putting on*
> *of apparel;*
> *But let it be the hidden man of the heart, in that which*
> *is not corruptible, even the ornament of a meek and quiet*
> *spirit, which is in the sight of God of great price.*
> *For after this manner in the old time the holy women also,*
> *who trusted in God, adorned themselves, being in subjection*
> *unto their own husbands:*
>
> 1 Peter 3:1–5

Ladies, please keep in mind that you are to be in subjection to a husband who is operating in love the way Christ loves the Church. Submission does not mean that you have to withstand abuse of any kind (emotional, mental, or physical). The Lord is not in jail for domestic abuse, so these men, especially men in the Church, should not be abusing their wives. Some women need to mix some wisdom with their love, and some men need to mix some Jesus in with their titles and positions in the Church. I can't tell you how many times I have heard people dog the wife and defend the husband. That is because of what they see on the outside. They don't know that this woman has been mentally and physically abused all week, which is why she doesn't make it to Bible study, but her husband does. They don't know that when she comes into the sanctuary looking mean and jacked up, and he looks like he just stepped out of a magazine, that is because he beat her in the car on their way to the sanctuary. That is why we are not to mess over the Lord's flock when they have been entrusted in our care. We don't know what it took for some people to muster up enough strength to even come in the sanctuary. We should be giving them the Gospel good news, not trying to drain them even more of their time and money, and having them leave the sanctuary in worse shape than when they went in.

I am fairly curious of whether these men in the Church think that God is pleased with them for the way that they terrorize their family. Why are some so quick to satisfy others outside of their family, but bring hell into their own home? Some of the deacons, ministers, and elders in the Church have seriously failed in the "ministry starting at home" area. It seems as if they would rather have their home in an uproar than allow someone else to get the last word because they are a "man" and the "king of their castle." How foolish does that sound? The King of kings and the Lord of lords left a wonderful example. All during His mock trial, He invoked His Miranda rights (before there was such a thing) and remained silent, because He loves us just that much. Why can't some of these men love their families like Christ loves the Church? Some men are so busy trying to be the king that they have forgotten and overlooked the fact that the king is to serve the people in his kingdom. If some of these men keep trying to be the king of the castle, their kingdom is going to have a population of one.

Husbands, become the spiritual leader of your house instead of just a figurehead in public, because women were not built for the level of stress that they carry. Women were designed to help (Genesis 2:18), not to carry the whole load by themselves.

> *Marriage is honourable in all, and the bed undefiled: but whoremongers and adulterers God will judge.*
>
> Hebrews 13:4

To the Parents—

Are You "In the Lord"?

Children, obey your parents in the Lord: for this is right.

Honour thy father and mother; which is the first commandment with promise;

That it may be well with thee, and thou mayest live long on the earth.

And, ye fathers, provoke not your children to wrath: but bring them up in the nurture and admonition of the Lord.

Servants, be obedient to them that are your masters according to the flesh, with fear and trembling, in singleness of your heart, as unto Christ;

Not with eyeservice, as menpleasers; but as the servants of Christ, doing the will of God from the heart;

With good will doing service, as to the Lord, and not to men: Knowing that whatsoever good thing any man doeth, the same shall he receive of the Lord, whether he be bond or free.

And, ye masters, do the same things unto them, forbearing threatening: knowing that your Master also is in heaven; neither is there respect of persons with him.

*Finally, my brethren, be strong in the Lord, and in the
power of his might.*

Ephesians 6:1–10

The Scripture says, *obey your parents in the Lord: for this is
right.* For the parents who are leaning on this Scripture for obedience from their children, maybe a reassessment is necessary on
the part of the parents to ensure that they are "in the Lord." A
part of this passage that I think bears repeating is verse four,
*And, ye fathers, provoke not your children to wrath: but bring them up
in the nurture and admonition of the Lord.* I can't express how many
times I have seen fathers (and on occasion mothers) provoke their
children and still expect obedience. I am in utter amazement
at times when fathers think that they can do and say anything
to their children, and the child is just supposed to fall in line
because they are the father. I don't understand provoking wrath
and then being surprised when it comes. There are only so many
times you can poke a rabid dog before it bites you in the butt.
When I say "provoke," I don't mean the fathers who are correcting their children. I am talking about the ones who instigate
their child's doing wrong and then chastise the child for doing
wrong.

With that said, girls and boys with parents *in the Lord* should
really try to look at things from their parents' point of view. They
are just trying to ensure that their children know the Lord and are
good people. Most of these parents are trying to impart knowledge, because they know that they won't be with their children
always. They want to know that when they are gone, their children will be able to take care of themselves, stand for Christ, and
know the devil even if he is coming as a wolf in sheep's clothing.

40

Real parents don't wake up every morning and say to themselves, "I wonder how I can mess with my child today."

All parents are not created equally. My heart bleeds for the real mothers and the real fathers, because they are dealing with a set of demons unlike any other. Not only do they have to deal with the demon that rises up in their child, but they have to deal with fake parents and their offspring. For those who are unaware of how to spot a fake parent, let me paint a picture. Fake parents criticize their children for being crooked, but they are not walking the straight and narrow themselves. In case anyone hasn't noticed, the "do as I say, not as I do" style of parenting doesn't work. Children are more prone to mimic what they see than to do what they are told. These fake parents say things like, "I know that they are going to do this anyway, so I would rather they did it under my supervision." How stupid is that? These fake mamas and daddies will allow their child to sleep around, drink, and do drugs under their "supervision."

People with a parenting style like that may need a little parental supervision themselves. When the real parents' child goes to school, they run into the fake parents' offspring. So now there is this little demon in the school telling these good kids, "My mom lets us do this and my dad lets us to that." Some parents won't even let their children go over to their friend's house, because their friend has these fake parents that allow anything to go on under their roof. When these children come home from school, they give their real parents hell. They want to know why they can't do the things that their friends are allowed to do. Children, these are some of the reasons your parents won't let you do what your friends are allowed to do:

1. Your parents don't want to go against everything in them to sit with you at an abortion clinic to kill the

product of your bad decisions (their grandchild, by the way);

2. Your parents don't want to cry themselves to sleep every night after the doctor tells you that you have AIDS;

3. Your parents don't want to struggle to tell the nice policeman at their door about the clothes that you were wearing before you left the house, because a body was found in a ditch and you are unaccounted for;

4. They are real parents, and not these fake, piss-poor, pathetic excuses for parents that are out there today. That's why!

A real mother is like the Syrophenician woman in Mark 7:26–30. This woman was desperate for her daughter to be healed. The Lord told her in verse 27, *Let the children first be filled: for it is not meet to take the children's bread, and to cast it unto the dogs.* The Lord was referring to the fact that He was there originally to provide for and endow the Jews (Cornelius's persistence opens the door for the Gentiles in Acts chapter 10). But the woman did not give up so quickly. She was concerned about her child. In verse 28, she says that even the dogs are allowed to eat the children's crumbs. Because the woman was persistent and did not leave because of the perceived offense, and she had faith in the Lord's power, her daughter was healed.

A real father is like Jairus in Luke 8:40–42, 49–56. Jairus was a man of importance, but that did not keep him from humbling himself and seeking out Jesus, so that his daughter could be healed. The Syrophenician woman and Jarius were not fake mothers and fake fathers…they were real parents who humbled themselves before the Lord for their children.

Train up a child in the way he should go: and when he is old, he will not depart from it (Proverbs 22:6). That Scripture does not mean that children won't think that the grass is greener somewhere else, but it does mean that God's got it. As long as holiness is instilled at an early age, even when children get in trouble they will know how to trust in God. Prayers of parents who are in the Lord will cover their children. But there is only so long that children can survive under their parents' prayers. They can't get into heaven off of Mommy and Daddy's prayers. They have to know the Lord for themselves.

The average amount of time that is spent in church is about four to eight hours in a given week (give or take a few revivals). One hour for Sunday school, two to three hours for Sunday morning service, and about an hour and a half to two hours for Bible study. There are 168 hours in a week. Hours spent in the church building are less than five percent of the total hours in a week. For the parents who are relying on the church building to whip their children into shape, don't be shocked if the child strays. Something has to be done outside of the church building. Parents need to be on one accord at home, so that they can instill something in the child at home. If the child is not strong in the Lord, one seven- to eight-hour day at school on Monday can undo a week's worth of church, if it is not being reinforced in the home. Parents and children, I want you to think long and hard. Which is best? By best, I don't mean the most popular versus what is going to make someone uncomfortable. I mean, who is the better shepherd/parent? The one who corrects, or the shepherd/parent who allows their sheep/children to do whatever they want, even though it feels good now but could kill or harm them later in life?

After all of that, I hate to end this section on this note, but some parents are suffering (mentally and physically), and they need some relief. There is a lesson that you are going to have to learn about your kids and about life. This is one of the first lessons that God had to teach me, and it was a painful lesson that I still struggle with from time to time. I had to learn that I am not God. I don't say that in an arrogant and narcissistic way. The lesson to teach me that I am not God had nothing to do with me thinking that I was above anyone. The lesson was because there was a time when I thought I could get anyone saved. I thought all I had to do was tell people about the Lord and let them know of His presence and awesome power, and they would be saved, and that would be another soul for the kingdom. But after being frustrated time and time again, God had to let me know that I was not Him.

He let me know no matter what I did or what I said, it was Him. If God didn't save them, if He didn't deliver them, they would not be saved and they would not be delivered. The first thing is that eventually they are going to have to invite Him in. I could not hold the door to people's hearts open and push the Lord inside. People have to know Him and accept Him for themselves. That lesson hurt so much. I desperately wanted people to be saved who saw no need for the Lord and His righteousness. I mean what do you do, but keep loving them and praying for them? Parents, I hate to say this, but after all of the parenting advice (harsh but with love), remember we are not God.

A more harsh truth is, after all of the praying and laboring before God and nearly dying in the process, some of our loved ones will still go to hell. Hell is going to be filled with somebody's mother, father, sister, brother, son, daughter, cousin, aunt, uncle, et al. Somebody is going to weep over their lost loved ones.

In order for the Scriptures to be fulfilled, someone has to go to hell. The only comfort that I can think of for the parents is knowing that, as a parent, everything possible was done to prevent it; and leaning on the Holy Ghost for comfort.

I am not saying that to discourage anyone or to keep parents from tarrying before the Lord for their children and trying to bring them into the knowledge of Christ. I just wanted to make some things clear, so people won't kill themselves trying to make someone else live right (I may not be a mother, but I know what this feels like all too well). For someone who doesn't want to receive Christ, the only thing that you can do is pray for them, show them Christ through your life, and hope that they will come around (or at the very least that God has a Paul moment with them to blind them so that they will later see the light). I hate to see parents try hard to bring their children to the Lord and then pass away. Afterward, when their children get saved, they say something like, "I wish my mother was here to see this," not understanding that their actions may have contributed to the death of their mother.

God loves us, just as parents love their children, but don't love everything their children do. God gives us free will, and no matter how much effort is expended, a child might still stray. This does not mean that the parents need to stray with them and start accepting things that the parents know are not right to stay in their child's good graces. Parents should be more concerned with staying in the Lord's good graces. Just as God constantly imparts knowledge and wisdom into His children, so do real godly parents. Parenting does not stop when a child turns eighteen or whatever the age of majority is now (the parenting approach may be different as the child gets older and hopefully wiser, but parenting does not stop), just as the Lord does not stop imparting wisdom and knowledge to His children after we have been saved for a certain period of time.

*The rod and reproof give wisdom: but a child left to himself
bringeth his mother to shame.
Correct thy son, and he shall give thee rest; yea, he shall
give delight unto thy soul.*

Proverbs 29:15, 17

To the Corporate Climbers and the Part-Time Christians in the Church—

You Have Got to be Kidding Me!

Some people might not know what corporate climbers and part-time Christians are. Chances are people have seen them, but didn't know what to call them. A corporate climber in the Church is someone whose focus is not on God, but on trying to get closer to the pastor and other people in the church who they feel are powerful and influential. Corporate climbers are chameleons. They will adapt to their environment. They will side with whomever they perceive to be the most powerful person in the room, and they will turn on that person if someone more powerful is to come in. They come under the guise of doing work for the Lord and wanting to be helpful, but they are trying to use their money or other resources to gain prestige in the Church. Some of these corporate climbers come to the church and think if they have enough money they can buy a church and a pastor as a puppet. The sad thing is that sometimes they can. So as long as they dangle their money like a carrot in front of a horse (the pastor or his wife), they think that they can do whatever they want.

47

There are also some corporate climbers in the church who don't have a lot of money, but they still want that next title and that next position. So they have to be a little bit more conniving because they don't have excess money that they can throw around. The less well-off corporate climbers are more or less cut-throats because they have to lie, cheat, steal, rape, rob, and pillage to get what they want.

Then there is the part-time Christian, also known as the Sunday morning saint or casual Christian. The part-time Christians are sometimes a product of the Church. Because of the lack of teaching and because the clergy is out of order, the part-time Christians feel that it is all right to behave this way as well. So they pretend to be saved on Sunday morning (and during Bible study, if they attend), and any time after that they "do what they do." No thought is given to the Lord or what He desires from us, unless they are inside the sanctuary or they need to put on airs for some reason.

Part-time Christians are more prone to try to get in their pastor's good graces because they have elevated their pastor above Christ, because they can relate more to the flaws in their pastor than they can to the righteousness of God. They seem to think that their pastor has the ability to absolve them of their sins (sorry, only God can). Since most pastors have become increasingly greedy, all the part-time Christians have to do is present the pastor (or his wife) with a gift, and the way that they are treated is like everything is fine. I dare anyone to say anything to them to the contrary.

Part-time Christians seem to think if their pastor does not correct them, then they have done nothing wrong. Well, the problem with that is so much is allowed in the Church now, with the pastor not batting an eyelash, that only the saved and sanctified are chastised. The part-time Christians are the "church folk" who will talk about the Lord and in the same breath cuss someone out for walking in front of the television during the game. Just to clarify, all part-time Christians are not corporate climbers, but a large percentage of corporate climbers are part-time Christians (the other percent of corporate climbers are really not claiming salvation at all—they just want yet another thing to get to the top of the ladder of and control).

These corporate climbers have no regard for God, but they can quote the Bible like nobody's business. They are like it says in 2 Timothy 3:5: *Having a form of godliness, but denying the power thereof: from such turn away.* Does this bear resemblance to someone else? Probably to the angel that was cast out of heaven when he started to get a little too big for his britches. Well, the corporate climbers in the Church bear some of Lucifer's likeness. Corporate climbers seem to think that they have a lot to teach and nothing to learn. I liken them sometimes to Romans 1:21–23:

> *Because that, when they knew God, they glorified him not as God, neither were thankful; but became vain in their imaginations, and their foolish heart was darkened. Professing themselves to be wise, they became fools, And changed the glory of the uncorruptible God into an image made like to corruptible man, and to birds, and fourfooted beasts, and creeping things.*

Corporate climbers don't even listen to anyone, unless that person has a title higher than their own. 1 Peter 5:5 tells us that we are to humble ourselves to one another. Just because the pastor or someone of a high status and title in the Church is not the one doing the correcting, that does not mean that correction can be ignored. Most corporate climbers are draped with titles and positions and have no substance. They will crawl in the sanctuary on bloody nubs, half dead, if asked to preach or do anything that would put the spotlight on them, but they have no true relationship with the Lord (that doesn't mean they can't fake it, but it is not real). If corporate climbers have their eyes set on a position or a title in the church, they go after it full force, and nothing can get in their way. God help you if you are the individual who has the title or position they want. They will lie about you and try to discredit you to get what you have. Whatever happened to Proverbs 18:16? The Bible says, *A man's gift maketh room for him, and bringeth him before great men.* If a person is truly gifted in something other than manipulation, chaos, and confusion, and they believe the Word, they don't have to do all of that to gain prominence.

What the corporate climbers fail to realize is that there are some bishops, elders, deacons, and evangelists going to hell. A title and a position in the Church does not provide any additional favor to get into heaven. The entrance criteria to get into heaven is not money, status, title, position, or anything else that man can give. Everything that these corporate climbers are doing is for nothing. It is not the key to heaven. Not only will that stuff not help anyone get into heaven, but the "good deeds" that were done won't even count when standing before the Lord on the Day of Judgment, because they were not done to hear from heaven, but to be seen of men. There is no double dipping when it comes to things of God. The Bible clearly states in Matthew 6 that when giving, fasting, and praying is done to be seen of men, then that person has already received their reward, so a reward should not be expected yet again from our heavenly Father.

Corporate climbers have a tendency to suffer from the "look at me" syndrome. They give so that they can get up and testify that they did so, but the Bible says in Matthew 6:2, *Therefore when thou doest thine alms, do not sound a trumpet before thee, as the hypocrites do in the synagogues and in the streets, that they may have glory of men. Verily I say unto you, They have their reward.* They pray long and loud, not to uplift the Lord, but again to be seen of men. Matthew 6:5 says, *And when thou prayest, thou shalt not be as the hypocrites are: for they love to pray standing in the synagogues and in the corners of the streets, that they may be seen of men. Verily I say unto you, They have their reward.* They fast so that people can look at them and say, "Man, aren't they saved." But they are not truly saved according to Matthew 6:16: *Moreover when ye fast, be not, as the hypocrites, of a sad countenance: for they disfigure their faces, that they may appear unto men to fast. Verily I say unto you, They have their reward.* Genuine giving, praying, and fasting are done according to Matthew 6:3–4, 6–7, 17–18. They are done for the glory of God and not to be seen of men.

Corporate climbers think that they are above correction. According to the Bible, *nobody* is above correction, no matter what their title and their position is:

> And ye have forgotten the exhortation which speaketh unto you as unto children, My son, despise not thou the chastening of the Lord, nor faint when thou art rebuked of him:
> For whom the Lord loveth he chasteneth, and scourgeth every son whom he receiveth.
> If ye endure chastening, God dealeth with you as with sons; for what son is he whom the father chasteneth not?
> But if ye be without chastisement, whereof all are partakers, then are ye bastards, and not sons.

Furthermore we have had fathers of our flesh which corrected us, and we gave them reverence: shall we not much rather be in subjection unto the Father of spirits, and live? For they verily for a few days chastened us after their own pleasure; but he for our profit, that we might be partakers of his holiness.

Now no chastening for the present seemeth to be joyous, but grievous: nevertheless afterward it yieldeth the peaceable fruit of righteousness unto them which are exercised thereby.

Hebrews 12:5–11

In summation: we are to receive correction from our Father. If we don't, we will no longer be sons (and daughters) of the King, but we shall be considered bastards (verse 8). The last time I checked, the legitimate children of God are the ones who inherit the kingdom of heaven. Who are we to dismiss the chastening of God because it was not delivered from someone with high status in the Church?

The Scripture informs us that we are to receive correction, but it does not say that only a select few have to abide by the correction, and the Scripture does not state that only a select few can dispense it. All through the Bible God uses different kinds of things and people to get His point across. He uses a talking donkey for Balaam (Numbers 22:23–41); servants and messengers for Naaman (2 Kings 5:1–19); and, someone we would consider a whore today, the Samaritan woman at the well with Christ who went back and told the people of her village about the Lord (John 4:1–42). So who do these people think they are to refuse correction, because it is not coming directly from the Bishop himself? God can use anyone or anything, and the fact that some people think that they are above correction, unless it is dispensed by certain people, is disturbing. How many people in the Bible would have missed their blessings if they would have had this mind-set?

I grew up with both of my parents in the house, so I don't know what it is like to be disowned, but I know that being disowned from earthly parents is an entirely different situation than God disowning me. If I were given the choice of who I would rather be chastened by, it would be my parents, because being chastened by God can be quite painful sometimes. However, if given the ultimatum of being considered a bastard and missing out on my inheritance from my parents, or, instead, missing out on my inheritance from God, I would choose to miss out on my inheritance from my parents. Although I love my parents, the inheritance that my heavenly Father has for me far outweighs what I could receive down here on this earth.

In John Milton's *Paradise Lost*, Satan makes the statement, "Better to reign in Hell than serve in Heaven." Oddly enough, some corporate climbers are of this mind-set. What some fail to realize is that people don't reign in hell—they burn in hell. That tidbit of information would serve people well to remember. It is on rare occasion that a doctor, lawyer, et al., would be satisfied with being referred to as brother and sister in the Church. Celebrities, CEOs, presidents of companies, doctors, lawyers, et al., can't fathom reigning in the world and serving in the Church, so they have to have an equivalent title in the Church to match the one that they have in the world. These corporate climbers are no different than Simon the sorcerer who tries to buy holiness (Acts 8:9–25), but we were not purchased with corruptible things such as silver and gold. We were bought with the blood of the lamb. When Simon tries to buy the gift of the Holy Ghost, he is swiftly rebuked. *But Peter said unto him, Thy money perish with thee, because thou hast thought that the gift of God may be purchased with money. Thou hast neither part nor lot in this matter: for thy heart is not right in the sight of God* (Acts 8:20–21). Where is the rebuke for unrighteousness now? Where is the correction in the Lord's house today?

These corporate climbers look right on the outside, but they are wicked and rotten to the core on the inside. Matthew 23:25–26 says, *Woe unto you, scribes and Pharisees, hypocrites! for ye make clean the outside of the cup and of the platter, but within they are full of extortion and excess. Thou blind Pharisee, cleanse first that which is within the cup and platter, that the outside of them may be clean also.* The inside is what counts in the end. The portrayal on the outside only fools the other fools around you.

I was listening to the television while getting dressed for church one morning (I listen to a lot of television while getting dressed on Sunday morning) and I heard the late Bishop G. E. Patterson say something that was very profound to me. He was preaching from Judges 1:1–9. This passage of Scripture is after Joshua had died, and the children of Israel were wondering who to send first against the Canaanites. God told them to send Judah, and that the battle was already won. Judah then goes to Simeon and asks him and his tribe to go up with him. Bishop Patterson broke it down further. He pointed out that Judah means "praise" and Simeon means "he heareth." The first to go up is praise (Judah), and praise is followed by Him hearing (Simeon). Bishop Patterson later said something that has stayed with me. He said, "What good is your praise if the Lord don't hear it?" All of this faking that is going on in the Church is for naught. God does not hear praise that is given unto men. He hears genuine praise that is offered up to Him. John 4:23–24 says, *But the hour cometh, and now is, when the true worshippers shall worship the Father in spirit and in truth: for the Father seeketh such to worship him. God is a Spirit:*

and they that worship him must worship him in spirit and in truth. So why bother? If it is praise to men instead of God, why bother with that unnecessary and fruitless praise?

All I can say concerning the part-time Christians (aka Sunday morning saints): pray that the Lord cracks the sky fifteen minutes into praise service on Sunday morning, because if He comes on Tuesday, some folks might not make it.

> *But God said unto him, Thou fool, this night thy soul*
> *shall be required of thee: then whose shall those things be,*
> *which thou hast provided?*
> *So is he that layeth up treasure for himself, and is not rich*
> *toward God.*
>
> Luke 12:20–21

To the Sinners —

Choose You This Day Whom Ye Will Serve

Before I get started in this section, I would like to extend a heart-felt apology on behalf of the pastors and ministers of the Gospel. I would like to say "I'm sorry" for this "Church better have my money" gospel that is being preached now. We have spent so much time preaching health, wealth, and prosperity, and so many have neglected to preach the life, death, burial, and resurrection of Christ. It has been preached that if you pay your tithes and put enough additional money in the collection plate, this will absolve you of your sins—but that is not true. Only the blood of Jesus can do that. We have neglected to provide instructions on how to get to heaven, which is to turn right on Jesus's court and go straight (it is a narrow street, but you can make it). For the overall failure of the clergy to meet the needs of the people's souls, I offer my sincere apology.

Some of the things that I have discussed thus far probably have people thinking that they don't want the Lord, and they don't want to be associated with His Church. I would like to caution people not to equate what goes on in the church building with how God really is. People do foolish things for stupid reasons, even in the Church, but our ways are not God's ways (Isaiah 55:8–9), so don't confuse the two. Don't perish for eternity because of others' actions. I would not go to jail for some-one else, so common sense would dictate that I would not go to hell because of someone else either.

I don't want people thinking that they don't need God, and that they would rather stay in sin, but as the progression of the book continues, things may only get worse, as I continue to remove the cloak that has been over the Church for years. There are some things that need to be understood. Just because other people are crooked, that does not give anyone else the green light to be crooked as well. Man should not be the measurement of goodness. God is the measurement of goodness.

You have to remember that there is nothing pure in this world. If there is a way for people to gain power and make money off something, they will try the easiest and quickest way to that end. But that does not mean that God is not real. People misuse the Bible, but that does not mean that the Bible is not the Word of God. Remember, people will disappoint, but the Word will not return void (Isaiah 55:11). A sinner can preach you to sal-vation, but if that sinner doesn't get right with God, they will go to hell with the rest of the sinners. Yes, I said it, *hell*. People are not really familiar with that word anymore. I guess from the viewpoint of these pastors, telling people if they don't get right that they are going to hell is like telling them a bad fortune when you read their palm. They stop coming back for more readings, which equates to less money. Preaching the truth is bad for busi-ness. But there is a heaven and there is a hell, and one day we will all spend eternity in one or the other. So today is as good as any to choose whether or not to serve the Lord.

I have a question. Has anyone ever wondered why preachers have stopped preaching against homosexuality? I guess when homo-sexuality made its way to the pulpit, preachers were hesitant to preach against the actions of themselves or their colleagues. We treat homosexuality as if it were the sin for which God sent out a memo and said that this sin is acceptable now. He didn't, and it isn't.

> *For if God spared not the angels that sinned, but cast them down to hell, and delivered them into chains of darkness, to be reserved unto judgment;*
> *And spared not the old world, but saved Noah the eighth person, a preacher of righteousness, bringing in the flood upon the world of the ungodly;*
> *And turning the cities of Sodom and Gomorrha into ashes condemned them with an overthrow, making them an ensample unto those that after should live ungodly;*
>
> 2 Peter 2:4–6

God did not spare the angels for siding with Lucifer, He did not spare the sinners in Noah's time, and he did not spare Sodom and Gomorrha for the rampant homosexuality and all manners of godlessness that was going on in those cities. God is the same yesterday, today, and forevermore (Hebrews 13:8). God is not a man, that He should lie, nor the son of man, that He should repent (Numbers 23:19). So since God is the same and He did not spare sinners, how is it that we think He will spare those who are engaging in these behaviors now? God does not change! We change, the world changes, but God stays the same. We have allowed this spirit into the Church to set up shop, and it has confused people. Some seem to think just because the homosexuals are in the choir and in the pulpit, that homosexuality is tolerable within the Church. Since they think the Church tolerates it, they make the assumption that God is pleased. He is *not*. In the Bible homosexuality is not just a sin, but it is also an abomination. Just because people in the Church bless something or turn a blind eye to it does not mean that God is pleased. All of those who blessed the sin or remained silent about it will answer for their actions, or lack thereof, on the Day of Judgment.

Wherefore God also gave them up to uncleanness through the lusts of their own hearts, to dishonour their own bodies between themselves:

Who changed the truth of God into a lie, and worshipped and served the creature more than the Creator, who is blessed for ever. Amen.

For this cause God gave them up unto vile affections: for even their women did change the natural use into that which is against nature:

And likewise also the men, leaving the natural use of the woman, burned in their lust one toward another; men with men working that which is unseemly, and receiving in themselves that recompence of their error which was meet.

And even as they did not like to retain God in their knowledge, God gave them over to a reprobate mind, to do those things which are not convenient;

Being filled with all unrighteousness, fornication, wickedness, covetousness, maliciousness; full of envy, murder, debate, deceit, malignity; whisperers,

Backbiters, haters of God, despiteful, proud, boasters, inventors of evil things, disobedient to parents,

Without understanding, covenantbreakers, without natural affection, implacable, unmerciful:

Who knowing the judgment of God, that they which commit such things are worthy of death, not only do the same, but have pleasure in them that do them.

Romans 1:24–32

Not only is homosexuality wrong in God's eyes, but according to the Scripture it is also against nature and the natural order of life (Romans 1:26-27). That makes sense. If all of the species in nature were homosexual, this world would be a desolate place. Now people can go to sperm banks to reproduce, but animals in the wild don't. For the naysayers, yes, there are sexual organisms that reproduce differently, but, for the most part, the species of the world would die off. In the animal kingdom, identical sexes cannot mate with one another and continue on the species. They would become extinct. Some would argue that this is the way that some people are born. That is one of the main reasons why we have to be to be born again, because, after Adam fell in the garden of Eden, we were all born in sin and shaped in iniquity (Psalm 51:5).

Jesus answered and said unto him, Verily, verily, I say unto thee, Except a man be born again, he cannot see the kingdom of God.
Jesus answered, Verily, verily, I say unto thee, Except a man be born of water and of the Spirit, he cannot enter into the kingdom of God.
That which is born of the flesh is flesh; and that which is born of the Spirit is spirit.
Marvel not that I said unto thee, Ye must be born again.

John 3:3, 5–7

Seeing ye have purified your souls in obeying the truth
through the Spirit unto unfeigned love of the brethren, see
that ye love one another with a pure heart fervently:
Being born again, not of corruptible seed, but of incorrupt-
ible, by the word of God, which liveth and abideth for ever.
For all flesh is as grass, and all the glory of man as the
flower of grass. The grass withereth, and the flower thereof
falleth away:
But the word of the Lord endureth for ever. And this is the
word which by the gospel is preached unto you.

1 Peter 1:22–25

If we are not born again and we turn away from God, He will do to us what He did to those who turned away from Him in the Bible. He will give us "up unto vile affections" and turn us over unto a "reprobate mind." Take a look around. People have begun to turn away from God, and we are once again going to vile affections and being turned over to reprobate minds.

Sin is sin. There is no such thing as a Christian homosexual, just like there is no such thing as a Christian adulterer. Those two words don't go together. Amos 3:3 states, *Can two walk together, except they be agreed?* God has not agreed to walk with any man in sin. This is why Adam and Eve had to leave the Garden of Eden. They had sinned against God. That bridge was not fixed until Jesus died for our sins. God is pure holiness. If I were in sin and tried to touch God, I would contaminate Him. He will not walk with me for committing the same sin as someone else just because He favors me. Sin is sin no matter who commits it. If I were in sin, that sin does not automatically become tolerable in the sight of God or moved over into the gray area just for me. Sin is sin.

God loves the homosexual as any other sinner, but He does not love the sin. I know people don't like to hear that, because we live in a world in which everybody does whatever satisfies them, right or wrong, and society accepts it. I would probably be branded a homophobic person or a bigot because I don't go with the flow of society on this issue. But I am not homophobic. A phobia has the connotation of fear. I don't fear homosexuals, nor do I fear homosexuality. However, I do believe that homosexuality is wrong. I don't mind whatever stigma I am branded with for siding with the Word on this issue. But, in the midst of all of this, don't get confused. My example here is mainly about homosexuals, but don't be fooled. We eventually want to get on that holy train and that train don't take no homosexuals, no liars, or no other sinners either.*

Life is just a fleeting experience, but the Word of God will last forever. But just because the Word of God will last forever does not mean that we will last on this earth forever as well. Some people say that they will turn to God after they get a certain age or achieve a certain amount in life. Tomorrow is not promised, and we are to seek the Lord while He can yet be found (Isaiah 55:6). I have talked to a lot of people, and they seem to think that because God is so merciful that there is no way that He would cast them into hell. It is sad that people are of this mind-set. Others get defensive when people try to witness to them, and they like to say, "Only God can judge me." That is so true, only God can judge us, but I think that most people fail to realize that there will come a day when God will judge us, and what will He say? God does not grade on a curve, nor will partial credit be given on the Day of Judgment.

---

* "This Train," old devotional song

I was getting ready for church one morning, and I heard a story that so perfectly wraps up what I am trying to convey. Someone told a story about a judge, and I am going to paraphrase it. It started off with the judge on vacation, and he was out on his boat fishing. The judge saw a young man drowning and swam out to save him. The young man and his family were so grateful to the judge. They couldn't thank him enough. Then, as the young man grew up, he began to stray away from the Lord and get into trouble with the law. One day while he was in the courtroom, he saw the very judge who saved his life years before walk in and sit at the bench. He leaned over to his lawyer and told him not to worry, because this is the same judge who saved his life before. The young man stood for his sentencing, and the judge gave him a long harsh sentence. The man's family was in attendance in the court, and they ran to the judge and pleaded with him. They said things like, "We don't understand. You are the same one who saved his life before." And the judge replied, "Then I was his savior, but today I am his judge."

That story struck a nerve with me. I think about it almost daily, because that is exactly how the Lord is going to treat us. We are continually taught about God's grace and mercy, but preachers have a tendency to omit the part about God's wrath and His judgment. The children of Israel experienced His wrath many times in the Bible, but yet we rarely mention it in the Church now. One day we are going to reach for God's grace and mercy, and we are going to get His wrath instead. Right now the Lord is on the throne of grace. Right now He is our Savior, but there is going to come a time when the throne of grace will be no more and the Lord will be in the judgment seat. He will cease to be our Savior, and He will commence to being our judge. We already know what the duration of our sentence will be—eternity. The only question is, where we will be located to carry out the Lord's verdict on us? He is the lion and the lamb. He is meek enough to be the lamb that was sacrificed for our sins, and at the same time He is like the lion and ferocious enough to condemn us for our sins, if we do not repent and turn from our wicked ways. Some might think that this is an instance where the Word contradicts itself. In one Scripture we are told that God is the same today, yesterday, and forever, and we also know that at some point He will be our judge instead of our Savior. Well, that is not God changing—that is God being true to His Word. When the Bible says God does not change, that means that He does not go against His Word.

We cannot go to heaven dirty (in sin), or we would contaminate heaven. The Lord is coming for a bride without a spot or a blemish. He is coming for the pure and holy. A lot of people try to explain away by saying nobody is perfect, and they use Proverbs 24:16a to try to justify what they do. Proverbs 24:16a says, *For a just man falleth seven times, and riseth up again.* Yes, if we fall down we can rise up again, but that Scripture should not be used as a crutch. That Scripture is meant to give people hope that they too can get back in right standing with God. It should not be used as a means to live an unholy life and expect God to be pleased.

There is no guarantee that someone who falls from grace will have time to get back up. What if the Lord were to call you while you were in a fallen state? People who are in a fallen state when the Lord calls have a one-way bus ticket to hell. They do not pass Go, and they do not collect two hundred dollars. No, we are not perfect, but we are made perfect through Christ Jesus. Jude 24–25 says, *Now unto him that is able to keep you from falling, and to present you faultless before the presence of his glory with exceeding joy, To the only wise God our Saviour, be glory and majesty, dominion and power, both now and ever. Amen.* The Book of Jude lets us know that if we keep our hands in the Master's hands, He will keep us from falling. Then we wouldn't have to keep falling and keep trying to get back up before the Lord calls us home.

So, yes, I agree: man is not perfect, but we are made perfect through Christ. Not only can the Lord keep us from falling, but He can present us faultless (i.e., perfect) before God when we stand before Him on the Day of Judgment. If all I have to do to be absolved of my sin and exonerated at my trial on the Day of Judgment is to stay with Christ, then why would I not do so? Why would I risk eternity in hell? Why do people make hell even a viable option? To please people they really don't like anyway? I don't understand. Romans 6:1–2 says, *What shall we say then? Shall we continue in sin, that grace may abound? God forbid. How shall we, that are dead to sin, live any longer therein?* We are not to continue to sin even though we know that if we repent that grace will continue to cover our sins. God dispenses grace, but that does not mean that grace will not dry up on the Day of Judgment. The dispensing of grace is just to give us time to get right. The purpose of grace is not to continue sinning because we can reach for grace to cover our sins before we go into heaven. If we keep misusing grace, God is going to show us His wrath.

"The greatest trick the devil ever pulled was convincing the world he didn't exist." Most people would remember that quote from the movie *The Usual Suspects*[†], but it actually came from a collection of poems entitled *Le Spleen de Paris* by Charles Baudelaire[‡]. I have heard that quoted many times and in many

[†]   McQuarrie, Christopher. 1995, "The Usual Suspects." Gramercy Pictures.

[‡]   Baudelaire, Charles. 1864. "Le Spleen de Paris"

ways, but until recently I never stopped to think about it. That is exactly what has gone on. How weird would someone look now to speak of demons and evil spirits? We are rational beings, so, in our feeble minds, if the devil has convinced us that he does not exist, then he has killed two birds with one stone, because now it is as if we think that God does not exist either.

If there is no antagonist, then people reason that there is no protagonist. If there is no measure of evil, then people assume that everything is good. So when the devil convinces some that he does not exist, it has become increasingly difficult to spread the Gospel Good News because now, according to some, there is no bad news—everything is acceptable now. In looking at the world today, is there any wonder why the motto of the world right now is "sin is in"? Everything that is contrary to the Word of God is allowed with open arms, but God forbid someone walks in holiness and stands for Christ. The world is being deceived. But the Bible says in Revelation 12:9, *And the great dragon was cast out, that old serpent, called the Devil, and Satan, which deceiveth the whole world: he was cast out into the earth, and his angels were cast out with him.* There is hope. We do not have to be deceived. *In whom the god of this world hath blinded the minds of them which believe not, lest the light of the glorious gospel of Christ, who is the image of God, should shine unto them* (2 Corinthians 4:4).

One thing we are great at is justifying sin. Justifying sin has been turned into an art form. For example, sinners know every Scripture they think justifies drinking, but can't abide by the Scriptures that instruct on how to live righteously, and lay aside every weight, and the sin which doth so easily beset us (Hebrews 12:1). People in church will rebuke in public and repent in private. We are quick to point out what is wrong with others, but as far as we are concerned we are okay even if we are doing the same thing. But right is right and wrong is wrong. All unrighteousness is sin (1 John 5:17). This gray area needs to go away.

Sin does not automatically become acceptable because "special" individuals commit the sin. Sin, no matter what it is, does not move from wrong to the gray area just for me or anybody else. When most people sin, they say, "The Lord knows my heart." That He does. God is omniscient. He knows all. He knows how many hairs are on your head. That does not mean that we will be allowed to get into heaven if we have a full head of hair. Proverbs 16:2 states, *All the ways of a man are clean in his own eyes; but the LORD weigheth the spirits.* Our concern should be our spirit. We should not expend so much energy to get around doing what is right in the Word or to cover up our sin. We should expend that same amount of energy to get in right standing with God. When we are weighed, will we be acceptable in God's sight, or will we be found wanting (Daniel 5:27)?

Were they ashamed when they had committed abomination? nay, they were not at all ashamed, neither could they blush: therefore they shall fall among them that fall: at the time that I visit them they shall be cast down, saith the LORD (Jeremiah 6:15). There is no shame anymore. People do anything that they are big and bad enough to do, they claim to be "spiritual," and dare someone to say something about it. We have grown into the generation that does not know the Lord (Judges 2:10) and, quite frankly, don't care that we don't know Him. Everything is about pleasing our flesh, and we seem to go all out to that end. But this life, no matter how old the Lord allows us to get, is temporary. There has to be some thought to the eternal. We have to stop thinking about satisfying our flesh and focus on our souls.

Stop looking at the television and what celebrities think and at what they do. Most of those people have absolutely no morals at all, and for those who claim to "believe," they think that they can live unrighteous as long as they pay their tithes, and still get into heaven. Living like that is what the Bible calls *having a form of godliness, but denying the power thereof* (2 Timothy 3:5). I don't care what people say. When people say "I am spiritual and not religious," that just means "I know that there is a God, but I have not found a religion or a substitute god that agrees with my hedonistic lifestyle and will still allow me to make it into heaven." What can wash away my sins? What can make me whole again? Nothing but the blood of Jesus.§

Everyone has to know the Lord for themselves. We cannot make it to heaven without a personal relationship with Christ. I cannot ride anyone's coattails to heaven, but if I get caught up with the wrong people, I can get help purchasing a one-way bus ticket to hell.

To know the Lord for yourself does not mean that we can make up our own interpretation of the Bible to make ourselves feel better and fit our lifestyle. Christianity is not musical chairs. We have a tendency to change churches and denominations to find the one that fits us, because we try to get God to conform to us instead of us conforming to Him. We are not allotted the luxury to make up the rules up as we go along.

Knowing the Lord for yourself means that there is a personal relationship with Him. For example, my mother knows the Lord. I fully believe if she stays her course she will have a crown in heaven, but just because my mother will be in heaven does not mean that I will be grandfathered into heaven because I am her daughter. I have to know Him for myself. To make it into heaven, we have to accept the Lord as our Savior and turn from our wicked ways. Repentance is not just an apology, but much more, and it has to be

§   Lowry, R., composer, 1876, "Nothing but the Blood of Jesus."

coupled with action. Repentance is an admission of guilt, an apology to God for the wrongdoing, a belief that Jesus is Lord, and a turning from our wicked ways. Let me expound on the last part. If I were to continue to hit someone and say "I'm sorry" after each hit, my apology would mean nothing, because I am still continually hitting that person. But if I were to hit someone, say "I'm sorry," and then stop hitting them, then my apology would be genuine and sincere, because I am not trying just to cover what I have done, but making a conscious effort not to do it again.

Some people think that they can continue to live in sin, and then when they get old they can have their family around their bedside while they repent and make it into heaven. It's like they think that they will be the thief in Luke 23:39–43 on the cross next to Jesus who repented at the last minute. I think what people fail to realize is that everybody is not going to get a deathbed confession. There are some who are going to die in an instant. Those who remain when the Lord cracks the sky won't have a chance to repent because He is coming like a thief in the night (1 Thessalonians 5:2–4)—quick and unexpected, because no man knows the day or the hour. A choice has to be made. There can be no straddling the fence when it comes to the things of God.

> *And if it seem evil unto you to serve the LORD, choose you this day whom ye will serve; whether the gods which your fathers served that were on the other side of the flood, or the gods of the Amorites, in whose land ye dwell: but as for me and my house, we will serve the LORD.*
> *And the people answered and said, God forbid that we should forsake the LORD, to serve other gods;*
>
> Joshua 24:15–16

When we live in sin we are serving other gods. Joshua 24:16 says it best: *And the people answered and said, God forbid that we should forsake the LORD, to serve other gods.*

Holiness and salvation are a part of a daily lifestyle. We are saved by grace, and afterward we have to live in this world. How we live matters. *For by grace are ye saved through faith; and that not of yourselves: it is the gift of God: Not of works, lest any man should boast. For we are his workmanship, created in Christ Jesus unto good works, which God hath before ordained that we should walk in them* (Ephesians 2:8–10). Works matter after salvation, not before, because nice people go to hell too if they don't accept Jesus as their Lord and Savior.

I have heard people say that after being saved, it is okay to keep certain aspects of the unsaved life. I would agree with that some, but generally I would have to disagree. Yes, if someone is extremely boisterous while in sin, it would be foolish for them to become shy and timid when they become saved. But there are some things that cannot carry over. There is no "lying for the Lord" or being a "ho for the Lord." When we come into the knowledge of Christ and accept Him as our Lord and Savior, then changes have to be made whether they are mentally, physically, spiritually, and sometimes all three. In 2 Corinthians 5:17, it says, *Therefore if any man be in Christ, he is a new creature: old things are passed away; behold, all things are become new.*

People say, "Stop bringing up my past," but if no change has taken place, then there is no past, because your past is your present. If nothing changes, it will be your future as well. It doesn't take much to come to the Lord and be saved. All that is required is Romans 10:9–10, *That if thou shalt confess with thy mouth the Lord Jesus, and shalt believe in thine heart that God hath raised him from the dead, thou shalt be saved. For with the heart man believeth unto righteousness; and with the mouth confession is made unto salvation.* Be mindful of the fact that after the confession and believing, there are other things that have to be done to maintain salvation. Some people will say that all the thief on the cross had to do was repent and believe. That was true for him, because he died almost instantly after his confession and believing. But for those of us who don't die immediately after conversion, the Bible lays out how we are to live while we are on this earth. Stop being confused. Think about it. If all it took to get into heaven was to believe, then a person could confess that Jesus is Lord and then continue to live in sin. If that were the case, then Lucifer would have a place in heaven, even though he was kicked out. The Lord says that he beheld Satan falling like lightning from heaven (Luke 10:18). Not only does the devil believe that there is a God, but he has the boot print on his backside to prove it. Satan knows firsthand that there is a God, and Satan and his angels that were cast out with him will not be welcomed into heaven.

We continue to try to fill the Lord's place within us with the temporal things. That is the problem—it is temporary, and it will not last. In order to be fulfilled, the action has to continue. When we develop a tolerance, the action has to be done more often to get the same feeling as before. This is why Jesus tells the women at the well that His living water would cause her not to thirst any longer (John 4:7–14). He is not referring to the natural thirst that people have, but to taking His rightful place within her, then she would be able to stop going from man to man, or sin to sin, to try to fill the void that will only be satisfied by Him. We will all have to give an account of our lives one day, whether we are right or wrong, good or bad. *Wherefore we labour, that, whether present or absent, we may be accepted of him. For we must all appear before the judgment seat of Christ; that every one may receive the things done in his body, according to that he hath done, whether it be good or bad* (2 Corinthians 5:9–10).

I strongly urge all sinners to repent and believe. I hope that no one thinks that they have done too much, and God won't forgive them. That can't be further from the truth. We are all precious to God. Heaven rejoices when a sinner comes to Christ (Luke 15:7). There is nothing that anyone has done that God won't forgive, as long as we ask. But keep in mind that we are to seek Him while He can yet be found (Isaiah 55:6). No matter what, remember that God forgives. In Matthew 20:1–10, the Lord shows in a parable that workers who arrive at the eleventh hour receive the same wages as those who began working at daybreak. What that means is that a latecomer to Christ will be welcomed into heaven just as people who have been walking with Christ all of their life. But I would warn those who think that they will be able to calculate when the eleventh hour is so that they can jump in just in time.

A word of caution to the sinners who make the decision to accept Jesus Christ as their personal Savior: *Beware lest any man spoil you through philosophy and vain deceit, after the tradition of men, after the rudiments of the world, and not after Christ* (Colossians 2:8). Don't cave to the Americanized, capitalistic gospel that is running rampant today. Don't get caught up in the mind-set, "If God loves me, then I should be rich, have a big house, and fancy cars." The truth is that some Christians live below the poverty line, some are unemployed, and some may not have a dollar to their name, but that does not mean that God will not open up the gates of heaven and welcome them in with open arms. Don't get caught up in stuff and miss God.

> *Jesus saith unto him, I am the way, the truth, and the life: no man cometh unto the Father, but by me.*
>
> John 14:6

To Those Who Continue to Fight the Good Fight —

Don't Get Weary in Well-Doing

Don't be weary in well-doing. What a daunting task—to stay encouraged, happy, and filled with joy after being stepped on inside and outside of the sanctuary. There are many pitfalls that we as Christians should be mindful of as we fight the good fight. We are vexed by the things that we see going on in the Church, often we will have to fight without the covering of an earthly shepherd, and above all we have the thankless task of having to battle these false prophets who have ingrained themselves in the Body of Christ.

The business of church. Yes, I said it, and it is a business now. The Church is no longer a house of worship for all of those people who thought otherwise. The business of church should come with some type of warning sign for the truly saved. There should be some type of flashing light that says, "The truly saved need not apply." I am begging and warning all at the same time. Stay on the spiritual side of church (if there still is one in your respective churches). The business side of church will annoy the crap out of you. It will vex your spirit to no end. These pastors are building their churches on the backs of others, and when it gets to a level that the pastors are comfortable with, the people who helped build it are cast aside for the pastor's family and friends.

The Church has evolved into something that is just like any other business. What is the most important thing to businesses? Money, correct! How do churches get more money? They have to put more butts in seats or appeal to a wealthier clientele. There is no getting closer to God by doing the business of church. These pastors (or CEOs, as I affectionately refer to them) have started moving the saved and sanctified out of the way and bringing in the businesspeople and moneymakers (odd move for organizations that are supposed to be nonprofit and use the money that they do make to help others, but I digress). The pastors only go to the back and parade out the saved and sanctified when it is convenient and cost-effective. So now the hierarchy of the Church resembles the organization chart of a business. The pastor (or head deacon, depending on the denomination) is the CEO. Instead of the saved being in positions in the Church, the educated are. We have exchanged education for salvation. I don't know about anybody else, but I don't think that that was a smart or fair trade.

I guess some preachers failed to read Proverbs 29:2: *When the righteous are in authority, the people rejoice: but when the wicked beareth rule, the people mourn.* One translation says that the people are on edge. The true Body of Christ in most churches is in mourning and on edge. To all of those in a position of authority in the Body, stop putting the wicked over the righteous! I don't care what kind of talents they have, I don't care how much money they have, I don't care how well respected they are in the community, wicked is wicked. Wicked can come in all shapes and sizes: it can come in a sexy little black dress, or it can come in a one- or two-thousand-dollar suit. That does not make the wicked any less wicked.

The warriors who are still trying to fight the good fight have yet another thing to deal with in the Church that we see. Because the Church has moved to being a business instead of a place of worship, there has been a severe breach of trust. Most people have an inherent, ingrained level of trust in the Church. We trust that the wicked are not over the righteous. We trust that the whores are not over the single women, that the pimps are not over the single men, that the pedophiles are not over the children, and that the homosexuals are not in the choir and the pulpit. But this trust has been breached time and time again, until people don't trust the Church anymore. Now more than ever, the hos are teaching the young women how to be hos and cover it up, the pimps are teaching the young men that marriage is for later in life and they are to sow their wild oats while they still can, the pedophiles are in hog heaven around the kids, and the homosexuals are everywhere (some of them are even bold enough to get married so that they can have a cloak over them while they are in their sin). The level of trust is gone.

Then there are the false teachers and the false prophets. This battle is never-ending and will continue until the day Jesus comes back. The Bible tells us to beware of the false teachers and the false prophets, and to preach against them, because they have ingrained themselves in the Body of Christ.

Beware of false prophets, which come to you in sheep's clothing, but inwardly they are ravening wolves.

Matthew 7:15

But there were false prophets also among the people, even as there shall be false teachers among you, who privily shall

bring in damnable heresies, even denying the Lord that
bought them, and bring upon themselves swift destruction.
And many shall follow their pernicious ways; by reason of
whom the way of truth shall be evil spoken of.
And through covetousness shall they with feigned words
make merchandise of you: whose judgment now of a long
time lingereth not, and their damnation slumbereth not.

2 Peter 2:1–3

And the word of the LORD came unto me, saying,
Son of man, prophesy against the prophets of Israel that
prophesy, and say thou unto them that prophesy out of their
own hearts, Hear ye the word of the LORD;
Thus saith the Lord GOD; Woe unto the foolish prophets,
that follow their own spirit, and have seen nothing!
Likewise, thou son of man, set thy face against the daugh-
ters of thy people, which prophesy out of their own heart;
and prophesy thou against them,
And say, Thus saith the Lord GOD; Woe to the women
that sew pillows to all armholes, and make kerchiefs upon
the head of every stature to hunt souls! Will ye hunt the
souls of my people, and will ye save the souls alive that
come unto you?
And will ye pollute me among my people for handfuls of
barley and for pieces of bread, to slay the souls that should
not die, and to save the souls alive that should not live, by
your lying to my people that hear your lies?

Ezekiel 13:1–3, 17–19

Denying the Lord is a sure sign of a false prophet. In the sanctuary there are not many people who are foolish enough to overtly speak against the Lord, but the ones that we have to watch out for are the covert operators—the ones that try to make us think that the Bible is not relevant to today's life. For example, if someone were to say that Joshua or Joseph's life in the Bible were not relevant today, then they are speaking against the Lord. Let me explain. John 1:1-2,14a says, *In the beginning was the Word, and the Word was with God, and the Word was God. The same was in the beginning with God. And the Word was made flesh, and dwelt among us.* To speak against what is in the Bible is to speak against the Word, and to speak against the Word is to speak against the Lord, because He is the Word made flesh. Be careful not to be deceived. There is a difference between expounding on the Word and speaking against the Word. People who expound are the teachers that the Lord provides. Anyone who tries to act like the Bible is irrelevant is basically saying that my Lord and Savior is irrelevant, and they are a false prophet or false teacher.

From what I have seen over my short life, the devil does not have to work another day in his life. If he wants to derail a thriving ministry in the Lord, all he has to do is send in a false prophet with money. In no time that ministry will be wrecked and off course. Just one bankrolled false prophet can wreak havoc on a ministry. These pastors and other people in the church can't seem to look past the dollar signs and see the soul. The false prophets are usually the ones who put the most in the collection plate, or they have found some other way to make themselves seemingly indispensable. So now pastors have a dilemma. Do they stand with the Saints against the false prophets and run the possibility of their financial well running dry, or do they side with the false prophets? The pastors know where these false teachers and false prophets are, they know that these people are doing wrong, but they refuse to deal with the person, fearing that the false prophet will take their money and leave. So the choice is made: ignore what is going on and accept the cash. What kills me is that people have the nerve to jump up and testify that they have been blessed. They haven't been blessed, they have been bribed. These false prophets with money don't have to go through the pain of starting their own church and getting it up and running, because they can walk in and buy a church and a pastor as a puppet. What has made these false teachers and false prophets cause so much damage to the Saints of God is that they have embedded themselves in the Church. So, let the suffering of the Saints commence.

The faithful will face adversity sometimes just for doing what is right. In Acts 16:16–24, Paul, Silas, and Timothy are followed by a soothsayer, and she mocks them. When they drive the spirit out of the woman, the men who benefitted from her "gift" have them beaten and thrown in jail. Verse 19 says, *And when her masters saw that the hope of their gains was gone, they caught Paul and Silas, and drew them into the marketplace unto the rulers.*

We will receive our biggest attack when we start messing with what brings in the dollars (*hope of their gains*). When we start to get funny with people's money, then they start getting a little irate. We are going to be crucified for doing right. That is just a part of life. Don't let that keep you from doing what is right. In Acts 23:12, Paul was conspired against by a group of people who said they would not eat or drink until they had killed him. All Paul was trying to do was spread the Gospel, and that was why he was targeted. We are to *Rejoice, and be exceeding glad: for great is your reward in heaven: for so persecuted they the prophets which were before you* (Matthew 5:12). Nobody is going to skate through this life untested and untried. We have to keep our goal in mind. *No weapon that is formed against thee shall prosper; and every tongue that shall rise against thee in judgment thou shalt condemn. This is the heritage of the servants of the LORD, and their righteousness is of me, saith the LORD* (Isaiah 54:17). The Scripture does not say that weapons won't be formed, so get ready for them, it just says that they won't prosper.

The spiritual absence of an earthly shepherd is very disappointing, especially when trying to fight against the false teachers and false prophets. I've never been in the military, but I can only imagine the difficulty of preparing for war with no top cover. That is how it is now in the Church. Top cover ultimately comes from the Lord, but while we are here on this earth, the earthly shepherds are to provide some type of leadership in the right way. People have devoted their lives to God and to doing what He requires of them, but they run into problems, not in the world where they are ministering, but in the Church where saved people have become an anomaly. In this spiritual war, the generals (the pastors and ministers of the Gospel) have turned away, leaving the faithful to fight without the watchful eye and covering of an earthly shepherd. Without any top cover, we will end up like Uriah. We will be honorable, and in doing so be lead to the slaughter by men in whom we trusted.

Pastors, if you only knew. These warriors are primed to fight to the death for the Lord. They work not to be seen of men, but to glorify the God that we are all supposed to be serving. I get the distinct feeling that some pastors would prefer the false prophets over the saved and sanctified. I think that pastors are of the mindset that it is easier to teach a false prophet how to appear to be saved and holy while holding on to his/her wealth than to teach the saved and holy how to go out and acquire wealth. Let's not fool ourselves. We know exactly what these people are looking for, and being saved is not earthly profitable. That is what people want now. They don't want their churches filled with the saved, the holy, and the righteous. They want their churches filled with wealthy people—people with money and status so that they can compare stats with other pastors. The saved are like weird outcasts that are belittled from the pulpit to the door. Apparently the people in the church didn't get the memo that the goal is actually to be holy and not to fake it. The Bible tells us to turn away from those who have a form of godliness (2 Timothy 3:5). The fakers get praised, while the saved are ostracized. That's a little backwards, isn't it? But even with the ridicule, there are those select few who will overlook the ostracism and the constant belittling to continue to stand for Christ. These are the few warriors who can stand and fight in spite of their circumstances and lack of support.

Please keep fighting the good fight. As I look around at the state of the world and the Body of Christ, I am growing increasingly concerned. Teaching the Word in its true form, instead of mutating it to fit one's own needs, is rare these days. There are some people who are going to lift up their eyes in hell, who thought that they were on their way to heaven, because no one taught them any better. So to the warriors, I want you to fight on, but take care of yourselves as well. No one can raise Lazarus from the dead every week if they are not the Lord Himself. What I am trying to say is that you cannot hold a dead church on your shoulders without some assistance from God. You will die trying to rejuvenate dry bones by yourself (Ezekiel 37:1–14). We need the Lord with us as we soldier on. In most of these churches we are in a desert place, while in a building that they call "the Lord's house." It is easy to tell when it is not the Lord's house because there is living water in the Lord, and most people looking for the living water in the church building are about to die of thirst.

The warriors are suffering. The Church is a business, trust has been broken, there is no earthly top cover during war, the false prophets have taken over, and we are told that we are "back-biting" or being judgmental if we try to point out where the problems are in the Church. That's a load of crap. If someone steals from me and I call them a thief, I am not judging them—I am merely calling them what they are. There has to be someone who will stand and say this is wrong. That is why the warriors are here. To fight and preserve what is left of the Bride of Christ until the Bridegroom's return.

What is the alternative? Are we to sit back and do nothing? Are we to not flinch when these babies in Christ are being consumed one after another? Open your mouth and say something. Stand and fight. Yes, the warriors will suffer, but I would rather suffer for the Lord's sake than suffer because of something unnecessary that I brought on myself (1 Peter 3:17). Suffering is not new to Christians. The Bible actually tells us that we should be glad to suffer. *Beloved, think it not strange concerning the fiery trial which is to try you, as though some strange thing happened unto you: But rejoice, inasmuch as ye are partakers of Christ's sufferings; that, when his glory shall be revealed, ye may be glad also with exceeding joy* (1 Peter 4:12–13). All of 1 Peter chapter 4 talks about the saints and suffering. It's going to happen and there is no getting around it, but we are to continue to do the works of the Lord in the midst of our suffering. Galatians 6:7–9 says, *Be not deceived; God is not mocked: for whatsoever a man soweth, that shall he also reap. For he that soweth to his flesh shall of the flesh reap corruption; but he that soweth to the Spirit shall of the Spirit reap life everlasting. And let us not be weary in well doing: for in due season we shall reap, if we faint not.* God has promised the ones who continue to soldier on a most precious gift. But we can't give up. Longsuffering is one of the fruits of the spirit for a reason. Not only does God expect us to endure, but He expects us to endure like a good soldier (2 Timothy 2:3).

I can honestly say while I was going through trials and tribulations I seemed to always think that the pain was so great that I wouldn't be able to bear it. I rarely ever equated some of my trials of life to light afflictions, nor did I ever think they were as short as a moment.

For all things are for your sakes, that the abundant grace might through the thanksgiving of many redound to the glory of God.
For which cause we faint not; but though our outward man perish, yet the inward man is renewed day by day.
For our light affliction, which is but for a moment, worketh for us a far more exceeding and eternal weight of glory;
While we look not at the things which are seen, but at the things which are not seen: for the things which are seen are temporal; but the things which are not seen are eternal.
2 Corinthians 4:15–18

Without fail, the Lord always came to my rescue. He always came right before I thought I was going to be crushed under the pressure. Half of the things I have gone through I can't even remember in detail now. I look back and smile. I guess that is what Paul meant by "these light afflictions." They shouldn't even dwell in our minds because they will last only for a moment. How foolish would I be to miss heaven because of a light affliction that I can barely recall?

For it is better, if the will of God be so, that ye suffer for well doing, than for evil doing.
1 Peter 3:17

To My Brothers and Sisters
Who Are Living
Sweetly Saved—

Stay That Way!

*Know ye not that the unrighteous shall not inherit the
kingdom of God? Be not deceived: neither fornicators, nor
idolaters, nor adulterers, nor effeminate, nor abusers of
themselves with mankind,*
*Nor thieves, nor covetous, nor drunkards, nor revilers, nor
extortioners, shall inherit the kingdom of God.*
*And such were some of you: but ye are washed, but ye are
sanctified, but ye are justified in the name of the Lord Jesus,
and by the Spirit of our God.*
*All things are lawful unto me, but all things are not
expedient: all things are lawful for me, but I will not be
brought under the power of any.*
*Meats for the belly, and the belly for meats: but God shall
destroy both it and them. Now the body is not for fornication, but for the Lord; and the Lord for the body.*
*And God hath both raised up the Lord, and will also raise
up us by his own power.*

Know ye not that your bodies are the members of Christ?
shall I then take the members of Christ, and make them the
members of an harlot? God forbid.

1 Corinthians 6:9–15

1 Corinthians 6:11 says, "And such were some of you." *Some* of you. Everybody was not a ho, pimp, liar, cheater, and everything else, but yet we are made to think so. No, we are not saved out of the womb, but we were not ho bags and hell-raisers out of the womb either. We were born in sin and shaped in iniquity, but that does not mean that, as children, everyone was a hell-raiser.

Some people were raised right. Some children were actually raised in the way that they should go and never departed. It is quite possible to be saved at an early age and continue to walk with Christ. *And that from a child thou hast known the holy scriptures, which are able to make thee wise unto salvation through faith which is in Christ Jesus* (2 Timothy 3:15). It is also possible for people to be raised well, and the only thing that they are lacking in their life is Christ. There are men and women living sweetly saved and just don't know it. It is understood that nice people go to hell, too, so being nice isn't enough. But when these sweet people come into the knowledge of God, they are already living the saved life. They just needed to make that additional step and accept Jesus as their Lord and Savior.

For some reason being sweetly saved seems to piss off people in the Church. Just because some have done so much in the world and finally come to Christ, they seem to have a chip on their shoulder about the people who never left the Lord. The way things are going now, no one matters in the Church unless they were the biggest hell-raisers the world has ever seen. Don't get me wrong—God has delivered some mighty men and women of God. But sometimes people don't need deliverance from certain things—sometimes the Lord preserves them.

I was out of church one time for about six months. I would ask my mother if I had to go out and do something wrong, and then come back to the Lord, so that I could have a testimony and be an effective witness for the Lord. She tried to reassure me, but I just thought that she was giving me a "mommy answer" instead of a real answer. Then one Sunday morning I heard the late Bishop G. E. Patterson say, "There's nothing wrong with deliverance, but there is something to be said when the Lord preserves you." That did something for me. I came to myself and started going back to church regularly. Everybody does not have to go "balls to the wall" in sin and then come back to the Lord to have a testimony. I have one of the best testimonies of all: the Lord preserved me, and I am proud of that. Don't let people treat you funny because you were raised right, living right, and doing what the Bible says you are supposed to do. They are real quick to label you stuck-up and say that you think that you are better than them. Ignore all of this and be happy about being preserved by God.

I have heard people in the Church say, "Don't talk to me unless you have done something," or "I don't trust anybody who hasn't done anything." This is a big mistake, and it needs to stop now. This is how the Church has become one of the biggest breeding grounds for sinners. The Church is telling people to go out and sin and then come back to the Lord. How stupid is that? What moron who was so self-conscious about their sin came up with that crap? Who tells a person that you have to be a "balls to the wall" sinner first before you can be a Christian? But that is what people are saying, even in the pulpit.

These sweetly saved people are torn. Almost every Sunday they hear people belittling those who didn't dine with the devil at one point in their lives. To the sweetly saved, please stay that way. Do these people saying this not know that they are leading some people straight to hell? Let's assume that a sweetly saved person tries to go out and make a testimony. They go out and sin like never before. Did the people encouraging this ever stop to think that these sweetly saved people could die in their sin while trying to make a testimony for themselves? These babies could lift up their eyes in hell, and for what? To fit in with people who wouldn't know the Lord if He jumped up and kicked them in the butt?

Hear me and hear me well: everybody who tries to make a testimony for themselves doesn't always have time to get back to living righteously before the Lord calls them home. Please don't go out and try to conjure up a testimony at the expense of your soul. I know someone who, by their own admission, has been on drugs for over ten years, but there are some people who try drugs for the first time and die in an instant. When people are careless in what they say and how they treat people, they could cause someone to try to develop a testimony and die before they are ever able to get right. In 1 Corinthians 6:15, it says, *Know ye not that your bodies are the members of Christ? shall I then take the members of Christ, and make them the members of an harlot? God forbid.* Just be satisfied in knowing that the Lord preserved you and stay sweetly saved.

Some people may be jealous of your relationship with God. Instead of them coming up, they want to discredit you and pull you down. When these fakers and haters start coming out of the woodwork, just remember Jeremiah 20:11: *But the LORD is with me as a mighty terrible one: therefore my persecutors shall stumble, and they shall not prevail: they shall be greatly ashamed; for they shall not prosper: their everlasting confusion shall never be forgotten.* Fakers and haters are one and the same; when those who are faking see someone real for God they become haters. Ridicule hurts. I know, and I am not going to pretend like I am a machine, and that I don't hear the whispers when people talk about me. But just because they have already purchased their one-way bus ticket to hell does not mean that I need to befriend them so that we can get a two-for-one discount. Luke 12:4–5 says, *And I say unto you my friends, Be not afraid of them that kill the body, and after that have no more that they can do. But I will forewarn you whom ye shall fear: Fear him, which after he hath killed hath power to cast into hell; yea, I say unto you, Fear him.* My soul is worth more to me than fitting in. I have accepted the fact that I am different, people are going to mock me (even in the Church), and it is highly unlikely that I will ever truly fit in anywhere, even in the Church.

I know that the Church sends mixed signals. Whoremongers are glorified, and those trying to walk upright before the Lord are laughed to scorn. It is very important to remember that just because the Church is turning a blind eye to what is going on, that does not mean that God is okay with how things are. God wants us to be pure. God wants us to be holy. The Bride of Christ is to be without spot or blemish. Remember why we live the saved life. It is not to get friends or to fit in. It is so that when the Lord cracks the sky, we will be called up to meet Him. There are some who will succumb to the pressure and try to do what others do so that they can fit in. Don't do it. *Let not thine heart envy sinners: but be thou in the fear of the LORD all the day long* (Proverbs 23:17) and *Be not thou envious against evil men, neither desire to be with them* (Proverbs 24:1). Our bodies are to be *a living sacrifice, holy, acceptable unto God, which is your reasonable service* (Romans 12:1). It really makes me sick for people to say that saved folks are trying to be holier-than-thou. Last time I checked, I was mandated in Leviticus 11:44-45 and 1 Peter 1:16 to be holy because the Lord my God is holy. There is no way that I would ever be holier than Him, but holiness is to be my daily goal.

There is a story of the prodigal son in the Bible. Each time I have heard someone preach a message about it, the son who stayed is always vilified. There is nothing wrong with staying home and not straying away from the Father. Just don't let the anger of the ones who strayed consume you to the point where you cannot appreciate what the Father has for you.

> *And he was angry, and would not go in: therefore came his father out, and intreated him.*
> *And he answering said to his father, Lo, these many years do I serve thee, neither transgressed I at any time thy commandment: and yet thou never gavest me a kid, that I might make merry with my friends:*
> *But as soon as this thy son was come, which hath devoured thy living with harlots, thou hast killed for him the fatted calf.*
> *And he said unto him, Son, thou art ever with me, and all that I have is thine.*
> *It was meet that we should make merry, and be glad: for this thy brother was dead, and is alive again; and was lost, and is found.*
>
> Luke 15:28–32

I am the first to admit that it is angering when the sinners are lifted above the saved. It is angering when more love is shown to those who have no regard for the Lord than to those who do. A lot of things are angering when you are living right and treated as though something is wrong with you. But please hold on to the Lord. The father in the parable said that everything he had was at the son's disposal all the time. Sometimes we spend so much time looking at other people and what they are doing, that we take our eyes off what is at our disposal.

The son who stayed home is not a villain, nor is he unhappy for his brother. I believe that he was just angry. Angry about the fact that he tried his best to do right and was always overlooked, but the one who had done wrong was constantly praised and pined after. The son who stayed home felt neglected by his father. He wished his father would have made it plain that everything was available to him from the beginning, so that he would not have carried around all that resentment for so long. The Lord lets us know up front that He will withhold no good thing from us, but at the same time we are told that it does not matter whether you start working early in the morning or if you come in the eleventh hour. Everybody still gets the same pay—eternal life. We are to be happy for our brothers and sisters when they come to the Lord. We are not to envy them while they are in sin, and we are to welcome them with open arms when they come back to the Father.

It has been my experience that people love you when they perceive you to be beneath them, but when that perception is gone they try to hurt you as much as possible. Others often see what is in you before you know what is in you. If they can't use you, then they try to kill what is inside of you instead of nurturing it. Don't let what you see fool you. You can't be a ho on Saturdays and holy on Sundays. It doesn't work like that. No matter what you hear and what you see, keep your feet planted and grow some roots in the Lord. Don't sway any way the wind blows. We need to live according to Ephesians 4:14–15, which says, *That we henceforth be no more children, tossed to and fro, and carried about with every wind of doctrine, by the sleight of men, and cunning craftiness, whereby they lie in wait to deceive; But speaking the truth in love, may grow up into him in all things, which is the head, even Christ.*

The only thing that you have to experience in this world is the Lord. For everything else use wisdom and learn from others' mistakes; don't try to make your own. *Therefore to him that knoweth to do good, and doeth it not, to him it is sin* (James 4:17). Don't compromise your morals and the things of God for the things of this world that are fleeting and will not last.

> *What? know ye not that your body is the temple of the Holy Ghost which is in you, which ye have of God, and ye are not your own?*
> *For ye are bought with a price: therefore glorify God in your body, and in your spirit, which are God's.*
>
> 1 Corinthians 6:19–20

To the Saints Concerning Sin-ners and Other Saints—

Correction Not Judgment

Let me make something perfectly clear. All true Saints of God know that judgment is reserved for God and God alone. But there has to be some correction down here on this earth before we stand in front of God on the Day of Judgment. In 1 Corinthians chapter 5, Paul is writing to the church in Corinth. Paul is specifically talking in terms of someone who is walking under the banner of Christianity and still doing wrong and giving the Church a bad name. He is not talking about the sinners that don't know the Lord. He is rebuking those who are *called a brother* in verse 11. But Paul makes it clear in verses 10–13 that the rebuke to the one who is within (a person who claims to be a believer and is sinning) should be different from the rebuke or correction to the one who is without (a sinner).

In verses 12 and 13, Paul reiterates that we cannot judge those that are without (the sinners) because that is reserved for God, but it is our duty to correct those that are within (those walking under the banner of Christianity). Paul wants to make perfectly clear to the people who are naming the name of Christ that there are consequences to soiling the Lord's name. Paul tells the people at the church in Corinth that he knows about the sinning, especially the fornicating, that is going on there, because everyone is gossiping so much about it that word has made its way all the way back to him. He basically tells the leaders in the church in Corinth that since they are there and are doing nothing about the situation, he is going to do something about the situation from afar. In verses 5–8 of 1 Corinthians chapter 5, Paul states that:

> *To deliver such an one unto Satan for the destruction of the flesh, that the spirit may be saved in the day of the Lord Jesus.*
> *Your glorying is not good. Know ye not that a little leaven leaveneth the whole lump?*
> *Purge out therefore the old leaven, that ye may be a new lump, as ye are unleavened. For even Christ our passover is sacrificed for us:*
> *Therefore let us keep the feast, not with old leaven, neither with the leaven of malice and wickedness; but with the unleavened bread of sincerity and truth.*

What he is saying here is that to keep the entire body from falling with one, the one is to be corrected or removed from the body. As he talks about the leaven in the bread, he is saying that if someone in the body is perceived as wicked, then the whole body gets that label (even if there is a little leaven the bread will rise).

Think about it. If one of the big names in the Church falls from grace, that has a bad effect on the rest of the Body of Christ. Everybody in the Church is not raping people, fornicating, committing adultery, being a homosexual, doing drugs, and other things. But if a high-profile person is caught in an act like this, the critics of the Church begin to equate one individual's shortcomings with the entire Body of Christ. If that were to happen, the Body would have a stigma on it for no reason other than no one stood up and corrected the sin when it was taking place, or as soon as they found out. Instead people turned and acted like nothing was going on, while they were all the time laughing and talking about it.

In 1 Corinthians 5:12–13, Paul says, *For what have I to do to judge them also that are without? do not ye judge them that are within? But them that are without God judgeth. Therefore put away from among yourselves that wicked person.* In short, Paul means don't rebuke the sinners in public and cover the "church folk" in private. Neither are we to cover any sin. What Paul says in verse 13 is that God will judge the sinners, and until the Lord comes we are to correct the infirmities in the Body (or that claim to be in the Body). The sinner should have time to get right, but when people are in the Church and are comfortable in their sin and have no desire to change, it is imperative that the real Church do something about it, before that one infraction becomes a flesh-eating virus that consumes the whole body.

A person's motives and mind-set weigh heavily on how the Church should deal with that individual. For example, let's say, for the purposes of an illustration, that a drug dealer and a drug addict come into the sanctuary. The drug dealer is comfortable in his sin, but he has come to church to find more customers. That drug dealer should be removed from the Body. Before the backlash begins, I am well aware that we are supposed to be forgiving, but the Bible does not tell us to be foolish. By allowing that individual to stay in the Body, we run the risk of that individual contaminating others and turning them into addicts. Should the drug dealer receive teaching on Christ, and should we pray that he be saved? Absolutely. But use wisdom. Teach and minister away from the Body. If the drug dealer is allowed to stay in the Body with the mind-set that he does not want to be saved, but he is looking for more customers, there is a great risk that before the drug dealer is saved, he could cause others to fall.

On the other hand, if a drug addict wants to be clean and has not been able, the Church is supposed to wrap its arms around him. The Church is supposed to do whatever it can to help. Will the addict slip and fall from time to time? Probably. But that does not mean that the Church should not even attempt to help get that person on the right track. *And if thy right hand offend thee, cut if off, and cast it from thee: for it is profitable for thee that one of thy members should perish, and not that thy whole body should be cast into hell* (Matthew 5:30). But even though the Bible says this, the congregation will be sacrificed so that the Church can remain politically correct. I am amazed at how we have an issue with removing someone in the Church who is detrimental to the Body, but we have no qualms about excluding the saved and sanctified.

The sinners, the backsliders, and the saved—oh my! When I say sinners, I mean the ones who don't know the Lord. The backsliders are in the middle, because they used to be saved but turned away from the Lord. The saved have accepted the Lord as their personal Savior; they have repented and have turned from their wicked ways. Each type of person is to be handled differently in the Church. The sinners are to be dealt with the same way that Jesus dealt with them. Sinners were handled with kid gloves. *Let brotherly love continue. Be not forgetful to entertain strangers: for thereby some have entertained angels unawares. Remember them that are in bonds, as bound with them; and them which suffer adversity, as being yourselves also in the body* (Hebrews 13:1–3). Once they are introduced to the Lord and they knew what they were doing was wrong, and they wanted to continue to do wrong, we are to still love them, but at the same time we are to remove them from the Body, so that we don't contaminate the rest of the Body. Enough of the Church being politically correct, and allowing the devil to seep in to contaminate the Body. If sinners want to change, and they want to be saved, then they are to be welcomed with open arms, but if they see the Church as a way to cloak their sin, or as a way to find other victims, then they are to be turned away for the betterment of the Body.

The backsliders are interesting. They know the Lord. They have experienced His benefits, but for some reason have turned away from Him. People walk away from the Lord for different reasons. Sometimes they leave the Lord because of something that took place in the Church. They equate how people treat them in the Church with how God is. Even though this is common, it is a pretty naive way of thinking, because if you think about it, none of us were saved the first time we walked into the Church, so it is very foolish to assume that everybody in the Church is saved. I don't care how long they have been there.

Some turn away from God because they went through a hardship in their lives, and they could not understand how God could allow such a thing to happen. But the Bible lets us know that the rain falls on the just as well as on the unjust (Matthew 5:45). Just because we are Christians does not mean that we will not experience the trials of life. The trials of life affect everyone, but how we handle them shows that we are truly Christians.

There are numerous reasons why people backslide and walk away from the Lord. As Christians we are to feel a sense of responsibility toward our brother or sister who walks away from the Lord. When a believer has veered off course and wandered away from the Lord, but sincerely wants to find his way back home, we are to follow Galatians 6:1–3: *Brethren, if a man be overtaken in a*

*fault, ye which are spiritual, restore such an one in the spirit of meek-
ness; considering thyself, lest thou also be tempted. Bear ye one another's
burdens, and so fulfil the law of Christ. For if a man think himself to be
something, when he is nothing, he deceiveth himself.* We are to consider
our brothers as ourselves and try to help restore them. A different approach is to be taken if the individual wants to go back to
the world, because they think that it is "more fun" than being a
Christian. There is nothing that we can do, but pray for them,
and hopefully they will make it back home before the Lord calls
them. The Lord is married to the backslider (Jeremiah 3:14). But
if the backsliders don't get back in right standing with God, they
will go to hell with the rest of the sinners.

The saved. I hope that everyone is aware that there is a difference between church people and saved people. Church people
have a relationship with the church building, but saved people
have a relationship with the Lord. We are to continue to follow
the example set by Jesus: just like He handled the sinners with
kid gloves, but the gloves came off for the Pharisees and the Sadducees, and they were dealt with. God did not coddle those who
claimed to walk under the banner of Christianity and who should
have known better. Those with a true repentant spirit are to be
helped back to the Lord, and those with a haughty unapologetic
spirit are to be handled bare-knuckled. If I were to get out of
right standing with God, I would expect swift rebuke from my
brothers and sisters in Christ, so that I could correct and get back
right with God. Any attempt to coddle me in my fallen state will
be perceived as joining my pity party, or as compliance with my
actions. We have to hold each other up. We have to be like Aaron
and Hur. *But Moses hands were heavy; and they took a stone, and put it
under him, and he sat thereon; and Aaron and Hur stayed up his hands,
the one on the one side, and the other on the other side; and his hands were*

steady until the going down of the sun (Exodus 17:12). The saved are to keep the rest of their saved brothers and sisters accountable for their actions or lack of action.

No matter what people say, remember that God said, *Be ye holy for I am holy* (Leviticus 11:44 and 1 Peter 1:16). Keep in mind that the Bible says about the saved in 1 Peter 4:18, *And if the righteous scarcely be saved, where shall the ungodly and the sinner appear?* We are going to scarcely make it in, so what of the sinners who don't even know the Lord? Teach these babies. Remember that judgment is reserved for God, and God alone, but if no correction is dispensed while we are here on this earth, then hell is going to be full. If we continue to turn a blind eye to the sinners, as well as to the saints who get out of line, then we are just asking for trouble.

> *For it had been better for them not to have known the way of righteousness, than, after they have known it, to turn from the holy commandment delivered unto them.*
>
> 2 Peter 2:21

To the Pastors and the Ministers of the Gospel—

What Did You Do to the House of Prayer?

And Jesus went into the temple of God, and cast out all them that sold and bought in the temple, and overthrew the tables of the moneychangers, and the seats of them that sold doves, And said unto them, It is written, My house shall be called the house of prayer; but ye have made it a den of thieves (Matthew 21:12–13). If this doesn't sum up the current state of the Body of Christ, I don't know what does. The house of prayer. The sanctuary. In their true form they are almost extinct. There are so many things that have contributed to the almost defunct house of prayer and the elevation of the den of thieves that I don't know where to begin.

Let's start from the beginning, shall we? All pastors and ministers of the Gospel should read, take notes, meditate on, and get real acquainted with Proverbs 29:2. Stop putting the wicked over the righteous! Wicked does not always come broken down with horns, a pitchfork, and a tail. The wicked are smart and they are chameleons that can adapt to their environment. It would behoove some of these pastors to get a spirit of discernment instead of an atmosphere of greed, so they can discern good from evil.

The Church should not act like a Fortune 500 company. I know that certain things have to go on to run a church, but it has gotten to the point of being ridiculous. The business of church has overshadowed the true purpose of the Church. In case the purpose of Church has been lost on some, let me reiterate it. First and foremost it is called the Lord's house for a reason. The Church should be where the people can come to worship God together. It is the communal house of prayer. It is the place where we should receive sanctuary. It is a place of refuge. It should not be a place of business, unless we are about our Father's business. Selling blessings, blessed oil, and prayer cloths does not constitute being about our Father's business. How dare anyone put a price on these unnecessary trinkets and pass them off as what the people need to be saved? There was a price for salvation, but God loved me enough that I didn't have to pay it. Where are the pastors? I am not talking to the CEOs here, I am speaking to the real pastors. Where are they? Where are the strong men who are to protect the Lord's house? These pastors have gotten so carnally minded that they are weak in spirit. Because they are weak, the devil has seeped into the Church unchallenged. *No man can enter into a strong man's house, and spoil his goods, except he will first bind the strong man; and then he will spoil his house* (Mark 3:27). It doesn't take much to bind the strong man anymore (if that is what you want to call him). A little money, a house, a car, sex, and voila! The strong man is bound and gagged and his house is ripe for the picking.

I wish these pastors would do a little more teaching (and not just teaching; it would be nice if they lived what they were teaching as well) on the Word of God and how to live saved in this wicked world. But that kind of teaching is not done anymore. Instead the teaching hinges on "nobody is perfect" and how to get rich and bring the tithe to the storehouse. No teaching is being done. People don't even know why they come to church, because we are preaching money and status instead of holiness and salvation. What really gets me is the ones who know and love the Lord are beat up in the Church. I never understood the belittling of the Saints in the Church. Who would mock a couple for being married for thirty years or more? No one would. So why would anyone mock someone who has been saved and walking with the Lord for thirty years or more? If someone has been saved for that long, we should be running toward them to see how they did it, instead of running away and laughing them to scorn. Those people are the ones who should be teaching in the Church. We need to hear from the ones who can teach on how to stay saved and holy for so long when you want to push the "Holy Ghost override" button sometimes. There needs to be some teaching going on in the Body.

It is sad when the children of God don't even hear about the Holy Ghost from the pulpit.

> *And it came to pass, that, while Apollos was at Corinth, Paul having passed through the upper coasts came to Ephesus: and finding certain disciples,*
> *He said unto them, Have ye received the Holy Ghost since ye believed? And they said unto him, We have not so much as heard whether there be any Holy Ghost.*
>
> Acts 19:1–2

The response to Paul after he asked have they received the Holy Ghost since they were saved was, "We didn't even know there was a Holy Ghost." Where is the preparation in the Church?

Where is the teaching? Paul is not talking to some random member of the congregation. He is talking to disciples (verse 1). Paul is talking to the very people who are to be out spreading the Gospel. How can people spread the Gospel Good News if they don't even know what it is?

If we don't speak about the Lord. then who will? These people in Acts 19:1-2 had titles and no knowledge of the God that they were supposed to be serving. They had positions and no substance. Stop ordaining everybody. If you are going to ordain them, teach them first. There are some churches that have more clergy than they do congregation. Some of these babies in Christ just found out that Jesus is no longer in the manger, and they already have titles and positions in the Church. Why? Just because the Lord called some people does not mean that He called them to preach. Maybe He was calling them out of sin. But these babies read two Scriptures and all of a sudden they are ready to travel the world and speak to the masses. They need to be cultivated and taught before the issues in this world overtake them and consume them. The Bible says He gave us teachers (Ephesians 4:11)—where are they? Were they kicked aside because they were not bringing in enough revenue? Where are the real teachers of the Gospel?

Would a man rob God? Hear me and hear me well. The tithe and offering is required by God. He does not condone the pastors and ministers of the Gospel misusing the tithes and offerings. The tithes and the offerings are to be brought to the storehouse, so that God's people may have meat.

Even from the days of your fathers ye are gone away from mine ordinances, and have not kept them. Return unto me,

and I will return unto you, saith the LORD of hosts. But
ye said, Wherein shall we return?
Will a man rob God? Yet ye have robbed me. But ye say,
Wherein have we robbed thee? In tithes and offerings.
Ye are cursed with a curse: for ye have robbed me, even this
whole nation.
Bring ye all the tithes into the storehouse, that there may
be meat in mine house, and prove me now herewith, saith
the LORD of hosts, if I will not open you the windows of
heaven, and pour you out a blessing, that there shall not be
room enough to receive it.

Malachi 3:7–10

The tithe is supposed to go to the storehouse, not the pastor's house. The tithe and offering have become the building fund for the pastor and a select few close friends and family. Yes, pastors should get paid. Jesus and Paul talk at length about pastors being taken care of by the congregations that they serve, but that does not give any pastor the right to bleed their congregation dry. The ultimate concern should be souls, not dollars. The Church is supposed to be there to help the people, not pad the preachers' pockets.

Have I committed an offence in abasing myself that ye
might be exalted, because I have preached to you the gospel
of God freely?
I robbed other churches, taking wages of them, to do you
service.
And when I was present with you, and wanted, I was
chargeable to no man: for that which was lacking to me the

brethren which came from Macedonia supplied: and in all things I have kept myself from being burdensome unto you, and so will I keep myself.

2 Corinthians 11:7–9

In 2 Corinthians 11:8, Paul says that he robbed other churches so that the church in Corinth didn't have to pay. Paul didn't really mean that he robbed the churches, but what he was letting them know is that he did receive payment from the other churches under his watch during times when he did not receive payment from the church in Corinth. Paul knew of the false teachers in Corinth preaching just to make a buck, and to not be confused by them and to continue to spread the Gospel, Paul declined any payment from them. Paul says in Acts 20:33, *I have coveted no man's silver, or gold, or apparel.* Can any of these pastors and ministers of the Gospel say that?

These pastors have become like the man who tried to build another barn to house his riches, and his soul was required of him that same night (Luke 12:20). These pastors have gotten pretty slick. I don't know who is better at milking people anymore, pastors or politicians. The pastors who are milking the most do it so smoothly that people don't know they are being swindled. The pastors get up and say that money truly isn't everything. They even preach a series on it once or twice a year, just to show that they are genuine. Just out of curiosity, if money isn't everything to the clergy, then why is it that the pastor miraculously becomes best friends with the ones who put the most in the collection plate? The pastor gets new pockets to put his hands in and the people who put the money in the collection plate starts to think that they have purchased stock in the Church. Funny how that works out. Maybe it's just me and my cynical outlook on certain things in the Body. These preachers know every celebrity, CEO, doctor, and lawyer in their midst, but they don't know that the waitress they had at dinner last night sings in their church choir.

My brethren, have not the faith of our Lord Jesus Christ, the Lord of glory, with respect of persons.

For if there come unto your assembly a man with a gold ring, in goodly apparel, and there come in also a poor man in vile raiment;

And ye have respect to him that weareth the gay clothing, and say unto him, Sit thou here in a good place; and say to the poor, Stand thou there, or sit here under my footstool:

Are ye not then partial in yourselves, and are become judges of evil thoughts?

Hearken, my beloved brethren, Hath not God chosen the poor of this world rich in faith, and heirs of the kingdom which he hath promised to them that love him?

But ye have despised the poor. Do not rich men oppress you, and draw you before the judgment seats?

Do not they blaspheme that worthy name by the which ye are called?

If ye fulfil the royal law according to the scripture, Thou shalt love thy neighbour as thyself, ye do well:

But if ye have respect to persons, ye commit sin, and are convinced of the law as transgressors.

James 2:1–9

I'm curious, what tax bracket do the rest of us have to be in to deserve an attentive shepherd? The Bible says that the poor will be with you always (Matthew 26:11 and Mark 14:7). Everybody can't be rich, but everybody can be saved. There are some people who can't afford houses and cars, they can't afford to buy themselves things like that, not to mention buy it for their pastor, but that does not mean that they love God any less.

> *And he looked up, and saw the rich men casting their gifts into the treasury.*
> *And he saw also a certain poor widow casting in thither two mites.*
> *And he said, Of a truth I say unto you, that this poor widow hath cast in more than they all:*
> *For all these have of their abundance cast in unto the offerings of God: but she of her penury hath cast in all the living that she had.*
>
> Luke 21:1–4

I don't even like to hear pastors and ministers of the Gospel tell the story of the woman who gave her last (Mark 12:40–44 and Luke 21:1–4) because they use it as a guilt tactic to get others give more money. Truth be told, that poor woman's gift would have been dismissed by the Church today, because she didn't give as much as the rich man. The Bible says in Proverbs 22:22, *Rob not the poor, because he is poor: neither oppress the afflicted in the gate.* Don't interpret this Scripture that you have to now stop robbing the poor, but you can still swindle the rich—that's not allowed either.

Being a pastor is supposed to be a calling, but it has ceased to be a calling now, and it is just another career choice and a status symbol. It has gotten so bad that now people are even trying to make it hereditary, like a monarchy, where they can leave their throne to one of their offspring. Let's be real. We have stopped building churches for the glory and worship of God, but these pastors have begun building shrines unto themselves. It is just something else they can pass down to their offspring. When a pastor starts to feel his mortality, he will grab his nearest male relative (e.g., son or son-in-law), and if he gets desperate he will actually consider leaving his church to a female relative. It doesn't matter what state is the relative is in. The child could have one foot still in the whorehouse or the crack house, and the pastor will slap a suit on the heir apparent and give him a title and a position.

Then these pastors have the nerve to do a preemptive strike so no one will question them, so they quote Psalm 105:15 and 1 Chronicles 16:22, *Saying, Touch not mine anointed, and do my prophets no harm.* But that is not really what they mean. The pastors have distorted that Scripture into, touch not my *appointed* and do my *profits* no harm. In order for someone to be a prophet today, they don't have to hear from God; the prophets just have to be profitable (or related to the pastor).

The Church has gone from prophetic to pathetic. Everybody is a prophet. Everybody is an overseer. Everybody is an apostle or this or that. Forget the titles—is anybody saved anymore? Does anybody love God anymore? Through all of the crap going on, does anybody even believe anymore? People don't care who they put over the Lord's sheep anymore. The decision now is no different from a board of directors picking a CEO who will bring in the most profits, and/or they bring in the CEO's son or nephew or somebody. Unfortunately, this is what the Church has become. How are we supposed to know who is anointed in the Church today? Especially now, because it is so easy for the wolves to purchase sheep's clothing. But as for the congregations out there, you better remember the Scriptures in the Bible about Eli and his sons Hophni and Phinehas. They had their father's profession, but they had no anointing, and God was not pleased with them. In fact, He was so displeased with Hophni and Phinehas and the way that Eli let them get away with everything that He killed all three of them and raised up Samuel.

> *Now the sons of Eli were sons of Belial; they knew not the LORD.*
>
> *Wherefore the sin of the young men was very great before the LORD: for men abhorred the offering of the LORD.*
>
> *But Samuel ministered before the LORD, being a child, girded with a linen ephod.*
>
> *Now Eli was very old, and heard all that his sons did unto all Israel; and how they lay with the women that assembled at the door of the tabernacle of the congregation.*
>
> *And he said unto them, Why do ye such things? for I hear of your evil dealings by all this people.*
>
> *Nay, my sons; for it is no good report that I hear: ye make the LORD's people to transgress.*
>
> *If one man sin against another, the judge shall judge him: but if a man sin against the LORD, who shall intreat for him? Notwithstanding they hearkened not unto the voice of their father, because the LORD would slay them.*
>
> *And the child Samuel grew on, and was in favour both with the LORD, and also with men.*
>
> 1 Samuel 2:12, 17–18, 22–26

If we keep testing God, it is quite possible that He is going to start removing these tainted bloodlines just to make sure the Blood of Jesus is not contaminated. It is understood that pastors want their family members saved. We all want our unsaved family members to be saved, but there is no excuse for trying to save one soul and damaging countless others in the process. This is not what the Lord was talking about in Matthew 18:12, when He talks about the shepherd who left the ninety-nine for the one. Before the shepherd leaves the flock for the one, he ensures that the ninety-nine either could sustain themselves until he returned, or he leaves the flock in capable hands until he returns. The shepherd is not at liberty to lead the ninety-nine to the slaughter just for the one. I have plenty of relatives I would like to be saved, but I will not sacrifice others' souls for theirs.

Stop covering up things that go on in the Church. People cover things up for two main reasons. One reason is they think that nobody knows about what is going on, and no one will ever find out. I think that mind-set is kind of foolish, because I don't know if anyone has noticed this, but word spreads through the Church like an Old Testament plague on Egypt. Just because no one says anything about it does not mean that people don't know what is going on. Silence is not consent, nor does silence imply ignorance of the matter at hand. Everybody already knows what people are trying to cover up. The more people try to cover something up, the dumber they look and the more people lose respect for them.

The second reason people cover things up is because they think that with enough time, they can fix it. Pastors, I need you to keep this in mind. Just like you tell your congregation that God will fix it, that goes the same for you. Covering something up to try to fix it yourself is just plain stupid. People will stay in their sin as long as no one says anything about it and pretends that it is not going on. Demons are to be called out, because if they are not, they will reproduce. If we keep acting like the devil doesn't exist, he is going to continue to enlarge his territory.

Here's a novel idea. How about being a real shepherd and protector of the Lord's sheep instead of playing these little childhood games? Childhood games basically have the same goal: the most points win. This translates to the Church, because now there is a little game going on with the pastors. There's no name for it, but the rules are similar. The rules are the most money, most members, and the bigger building wins. My life and my soul are not a game. Most of the decisions that pastors make are not based on the Lord and development of souls, but based on fiscal needs and retention of warm bodies. What is the measurement of goodness in the Church? The measurement of goodness now is butts in seats. The Church needs to be full. Nothing else matters. Church leaders need butts in seats so congregants can put money into the collection plate. How many butts in seats determines how big the pastor's house can be and how many cars he can have in the garage. When the measurement of goodness in the Body becomes doing God's will, souls saved, and the number of members living right, then the Body will begin to heal of its many afflictions. These preachers today don't want to do the will of God; they want to be celebrities and be rich and famous. They don't want to be true shepherds in the real sense of the word. A true shepherd is my Lord and Savior. He is the good shepherd. All pastors should pattern themselves after the wonderful example given in the Bible. Don't give me any of that "nobody is perfect" crap. We can all be made perfect through Christ.

*The thief cometh not, but for to steal, and to kill, and to
destroy: I am come that they might have life, and that they
might have it more abundantly.*

*I am the good shepherd: the good shepherd giveth his life for
the sheep.*

*But he that is an hireling, and not the shepherd, whose
own the sheep are not, seeth the wolf coming, and leaveth
the sheep, and fleeth: and the wolf catcheth them, and scat-
tereth the sheep.*

*The hireling fleeth, because he is an hireling, and careth
not for the sheep.*

*I am the good shepherd, and know my sheep, and am
known of mine.*

John 10:10–14

So, pastors and ministers of the Gospel, are you on retainer,
or do you care about the souls that have been entrusted to you?
Are you a good shepherd or a hireling? Is being a pastor a job or
a calling? I am very leery of a shepherd whose first priority is not
his sheep. God is concerned with what concerns His people. Are
you concerned with your flock? Or do you give them a pep talk
and tell them what you think that they want to hear so that they
will get away from you quicker? If you don't have the time for
your flock, maybe you shouldn't be a shepherd. It's funny how
some of these pastors find time to be on the radio and on TV,
but pawn their sheep off on the assistant of one of the assistant
pastors. If I wanted to talk to one of the assistants, I would have
joined their church. How about sending the assistant pastor to
be on the radio and TV, and you spend some time trying to help

the souls that have been entrusted to you? If you can't help the sheep in-house, it is kind of foolish to go looking for more outside of the house. If you can't meet the needs at one sanctuary, I don't recommend that you get a second or third church (or build a bigger one) to get more revenue coming in. How about you pay attention to the souls that you already have? Because knowing the poor selection of shepherds that are out there now, I'm pretty sure that there is more than one sheep that has wandered off or gone astray. Get to retrieving.

I am sick of these hirelings in the Church. I am not a shepherd. I am not a leader over a house of God, but I have the mentality of a true shepherd. I am concerned about the well-being of the Lord's flock. I am concerned when wolves in sheep clothing try to consume the sheep. I am concerned when one of the sheep is vexed. It is ingrained in me. That is why I can't understand how some of these preachers act the way that they do. If you are a shepherd, and you don't cringe when the Lord's flock is in trouble, and you don't try to do something about it, you should rethink your current role in life. Maybe the Lord called you out of sin instead of into the ministry. What happened to the Army of the Lord? What happened to the officers (the generals especially) in the Army of the Lord? Most of our generals have become defecting slaves or spiritual prostitutes. They have intentionally placed themselves on the auction block and sold themselves to the highest bidders. They try to convince their congregation that they are doing what is right for the kingdom. Is your anointing worth so little to you that you would sell it to the highest bidder? Where are the generals who can lead the charge to pursue and recover all (1 Samuel 30:8)? Not to recover all of the riches, but recover the souls that were overlooked for the riches.

I have heard preachers preach Matthew 6:24 so much that I can't count, and it has become a cliché: *No man can serve two masters: for either he will hate the one, and love the other; or else he will hold to the one, and despise the other. Ye cannot serve God and mammon.* The only problem is that I can count on one hand how many times they have preached verse 24 in its entirety. We naturally think that this Scripture is perfect for sinners, and it is, but it is also perfect for Christians as well. In the last part of the Scripture, it says that you cannot serve God and mammon. Well, *mammon* means money, or the god of money or wealth. So basically, the Scripture is saying that you cannot serve God and money.

I think it's funny how preachers never expound on that. Maybe it's me making something out of nothing, but I do find it weird that we have no qualms with telling people that they can't serve two masters and allowing them to believe that the Scripture is talking about God and Satan, and in actuality it is talking about God and money. These preachers won't teach about not worshipping money, because that is what they are trying to get. Way to go with manipulating the Scripture. The Scripture tells us that we can't serve both. Since we can't serve both, what has happened is that God has been evicted out of the sanctuary—a restraining order has been issued against Him stating that God cannot come within a hundred yards of the Church, and mammon has been welcomed into the sanctuary with open arms. In the power and influence categories, money has more power and influence inside the Church than the devil ever will. This is why greed is one of the most important and most effective weapons in the devil's arsenal. When the people tried to trick Jesus into saying something against Caesar so that He could be tried for treason against Rome, they used money.

Then went the Pharisees, and took counsel how they might entangle him in his talk.

And they sent out unto him their disciples with the Herodians, saying, Master, we know that thou art true, and teachest the way of God in truth, neither carest thou for any man: for thou regardest not the person of men.

Tell us therefore, What thinkest thou? Is it lawful to give tribute unto Caesar, or not?

But Jesus perceived their wickedness, and said, Why tempt ye me, ye hypocrites?

Shew me the tribute money. And they brought unto him a penny.

And he saith unto them, Whose is this image and superscription?

They say unto him, Caesar's. Then saith he unto them, Render therefore unto Caesar the things which are Caesar's; and unto God the things that are God's.

When they had heard these words, they marvelled, and left him, and went their way.

Matthew 22:15–22

While Jesus was rebuking them, He also made a good point. He showed that He was more concerned with our souls than with our money. Yes, we are required to pay our tithes (a tenth of our increase), and we are required to give an offering, but all of the other stuff besides that is getting real out of hand. There should not be a "spending money for the pastor" fund or a "the pastor's mistress's bills have to be paid, too" fund. Now people might find that a little funny, but if they knew where some of this money was going, they would know that I am not that far off.

The Lord asks to see their money. Caesar's face is on the coins. So the Lord says render unto Caesar what is Caesar's. Meaning, give Caesar whatever tax he requires for giving out his money. But the Lord does not stop there. He also says to render unto God the things that are due Him. What He is saying there is that if Caesar's image is on the money and they were required to give it back to Caesar, since we were made in God's image (Genesis 1:26–27), we are required to give ourselves to God. We were made in the image of God, and no matter where we are in life, we are not our own. So we have to live for Him and give ourselves to Him.

People say that there is nothing wrong with a Christian being rich, and that is true, but be mindful of how the riches were obtained, and don't worship the riches, because it is easier for a camel to go through the eye of a needle than for a rich man to enter the kingdom of God (Matthew 19:24 and Mark 10:25). *As the partridge sitteth on eggs, and hatcheth them not; so he that getteth riches, and not by right, shall leave them in the midst of his days, and at his end shall be a fool* (Jeremiah 17:11); and *For the love of money is the root of all evil: which while some coveted after, they have erred from the faith, and pierced themselves through with many sorrows* (1 Timothy 6:10).

We quote Mark 8:36 all the time. *For what shall it profit a man, if he shall gain the whole world, and lose his own soul?* But do we understand the implications here? Do we understand that just because we may rule in this world, it does not guarantee us a pass into heaven? Do we believe that money gets us into heaven? If that is the case, then all churches involved in missions outside of wealthy developed nations should stop, because the people in underdeveloped countries have no chance of getting into heaven in the first place. If it is true that we can buy our way into heaven, we should all go all out with all of this capitalism stuff and forget about Christianity. Forget our struggling brothers and sisters and their families. Forget about anyone who is in need spiritually. We are going to throw out the Bible, and every man for himself. Does anyone other than me think that is foolish? So why are we doing it? Why are we acting like souls don't matter, and the preaching from the pulpit is hinged on how the stock market is doing that week, instead of on what God has revealed through His Word and on constantly seeking Him? There should be no more Pentecostal, Baptist, Methodist, or any other kind of church. Now we are all fused into the Church of "Do You," where Bishop Moneybags is the presiding bishop, and the motto is, "It doesn't matter what you've done or what you are doing, as long as your check doesn't bounce."

Because of what they see on the television and the lack of real teaching in the Church, people have no true sense of what it is to live holy. The sad thing is the pastors and ministers of the Gospel are perpetuating the stereotype. Do they do things for money? Yes. Do they do things for sex? Yes. Do they use people and toss them away? Yes. Is there a genuine concern about souls? Rarely. Nowadays pastors and ministers of the Gospel are more concerned with being the most well-known pastor, the one with the most members, or the one with the most programs. We should be ashamed of ourselves. We should fall on our faces and beg the Lord's forgiveness for turning His life, death, burial, and resurrection into a battle cry for more money. Prosperity is not going to get me into heaven; the life, death, burial, and resurrection of Christ will. I don't need your distorted version of the Gospel, your politics, or your opinion—I need Jesus.

Humility should come before honor (Proverbs 15:33; 18:12). But a humble spirit is hard to find in the Church now,

because arrogance and greed reign supreme. Everybody is looking for honor and sometimes double honor (1 Timothy 5:17),
and they have walked away from humility. The level of arrogance
with the underlying greed disseminating from the pulpit is suffo-
cating. Since the head is contaminated, the body has become also.
I have never in my life seen so many church people be as arrogant
and greedy as they are now. People emulate what they see. If the
head is out of line, then the body will be also. The more I think
about it, maybe the Body of Christ has a severe headache and
the entire body is being affected. When the people moved God
out and moved their pastor in and began praising him, the Body
started having migraines, and it has yet to recover. The only way
to fix this headache would be to remove the pastors and put God
back on the throne in our lives. We have to let God be true and
every man a liar (Romans 3:3–4).

As angry as I am with the pastors and the ministers of the
Gospel, I can't lay all of the fault at their feet. Some of the responsibility for the monsters that are out there lay squarely on the
shoulders of the congregation. These pastors and ministers of the
Gospel will do what the congregation allows. The praise in these
sanctuaries is seriously misguided. Some of the people in the congregation praise their pastors more than they praise God. Then
they are shocked when the pastor isn't who they thought he was.

How is it that you will lose your mind for your pastor,
but when someone says clap your hands for the Lord, you act
like you are looking at your watch or going through your purse?
That is real backward, and it is a real problem. These pastors are
not developing soldiers for Christ, they are building an army for
themselves. That is why some people will fight to the death for
their pastor, but they won't open their mouths and take a stand
for Christ.

God inhabits the praises of His people (Psalm 22:3). But because so much of today's praise is misguided toward the pulpit instead of heaven, it is like God has nowhere to reside. It is as if He has to be turned away from the inn and sleep in the manger all over again. I guess I should leave the pastors alone. Like any other performer, they play to their audience. If people really want to hear the Word, the pastors would preach it. If people want to be told their fortune, the pastors will do that, too. If the congregation would stop treating these pastors as if they walk on water, maybe they will stop believing the hype and do what they initially set out to do.

Every pastor does not start off greedy and arrogant; some gradually get caught up and don't know how or don't want to come back down. The pastors allow outward praise to them from the congregation to get louder than the inward humility, grace, and Word of God in them. I have seen the most humble of men start to believe the hype and turn into glory hounds. Now it is next to impossible to go to some of these churches without praising the pastors and their wives. Some of these pastor's wives have a tendency to think that they are the baby Jesus, everyone else is the wise men, and we are to come bearing gifts every time we walk into the sanctuary. Think again.

When the congregation becomes the pastor's downfall, they seem to lift him higher than God and gradually stop worshipping God and start worshipping their pastor. The congregation normally finds it too difficult, for whatever reason, to truly follow Christ, so they find a substitute—the pastor. This substitute is praised like God, but since we can find flaws in the substitute, we have convinced ourselves that it is all right to have and keep flaws. So now instead of Christ being our measurement of goodness, the pastor is. Since man is our measurement of goodness, some perceive there to be room for error, since the pastor "isn't perfect," just like we aren't. But we are in error. Man should not be our measurement of goodness, Christ should be. Even though Christ did not sin, He took on all of our sins on the cross. So it is possible for poor little old me to be considered faultless on the Day of Judgment if I keep my hand in the master's hand. *Now unto him that is able to keep you from falling, and to present you faultless before the presence of his glory with exceeding joy, To the only wise God our Saviour, be glory and majesty, dominion and power, both now and ever. Amen* (Jude 24–25). So that "everybody is human and makes mistakes" argument doesn't hold water anymore. We are not perfect, but we can be made perfect through Christ.

Another big hindrance to the pastors, besides the congregation, are their wives. (There are some female pastors, and in their case their husband would be substituted; but there are not that many female pastors, so this section is written to the male pastors, but applies to all.) I have my own term of endearment for "first ladies." I affectionately refer to them as WoW. WoW stands for "witch on wheels." I have run across a couple of decent first ladies I have not given this title to, but for the most part it fits. There are a handful of exceptions, but most are either witches or witches in training. Here is a suggestion. Maybe when the pastor and his wife finish counseling others, they could get a little counseling for themselves. I'm sure your wife is nice when you are around, but did it ever occur to you that she is a witch when you are not around? In all honesty, your wife may be the reason your church has a revolving door. Most pastors would know this if they would just open their eyes. Now I am not saying that these pastors need to go home and beat their wives, and I am not trying to cause division in a household, but maybe one night while she is sleep you can roll over and ask the Lord to help you deal with your helpmeet.

Let's be honest—on occasion God will call a husband and wife team into ministry together. Notice that I said "on occasion." In truth He just calls the pastor, not their wives, too (at least not on the same plane). Wives have to be somewhat involved with the ministry, and they have to have an understanding of what kind of demands it will have on their husbands, but these pastors should not be yielding to every whim from their wives concerning the church that God gave them. I don't care how much they love their wives. God didn't call her, He called you.

It becomes very confusing when a pastor is trying to hear from God and has to also obey and hear his wife at the same time. The lines become blurred, and a congregation ends up with a pastor who loves God but listens to his wife instead. Esther did not rule with the king, but through fasting and prayer she was used because of her connection to the king. I am not saying that God won't use your wife every now and then, and I am not saying that women have no place in ministry. What I am saying is that each flock has a designated shepherd.

I wish that these pastors would stop lifting their wives up on the same plane as them. I know that they love their wives, and when they were married they became one flesh, but not in ministry. The reason couples are rarely called is because people are rarely ever on the same plane of knowledge and anointing in God. Don't get me wrong: if people have been in church long enough they can fake it with the best of them. But in order for God to use a husband-and-wife team, they have to be equally yoked. Not equally yoked in conning people but equal in the things of God (not just have equal titles either). Since that is rare, a dual calling is rare (not that some don't exist, but get real—all husband-and-wife teams don't need to do this).

After the pastor is comfortable in his position, he tries to bring his wife up to his level in his own strength, and that doesn't work. I'm not saying that the pastor's wife can't do things in the Church, and that God will never speak through her, but the Church has nothing to do with matters of the heart and matters of the flesh; it has to do with matters of the spirit. The divorce rate is the same in the Church as it is outside of the Church. Now I know that most pastors don't think that their marriage will break up, and I hope not, but if it does break up, does that now mean that the wife is to receive half of the flock that God has entrusted to the pastor?

The constant pull of listening to God or their wives (and no, God and your wife are not one and the same) will take its toll. Eventually the pastor may start to ignore God and listen to his wife just to keep peace at home. That is no way to be a good shepherd. The church, and especially the pulpit, should not be used as a marriage bargaining chip, nor should it be used as a therapist's office for the pastor and his wife. If there are any marital problems, they should not be taken care of during church service with the microphone. Take care of that at the house. If she has self-esteem issues or issues with anything else, take care of that at home. Buy her a necklace, make her dinner, break out your best moves in the bedroom, and be done with it. Move on. But don't use oversight in the Church as a bargaining chip to soothe things over at home. It is possible to be the pastor and outrank your wife in the church and still love her. You do not have to bestow the title (sometimes not even the title, but just the duties) of co-pastor or assistant pastor on your wife just to keep peace at home.

Stop trying to show your love by sharing your flock. The same way that you abhor it when your flock comes to you constantly with a "word from the Lord," your wife should be taken with that same grain of salt.

The reason I am harping on the pastors listening to God instead of their wives is because I have seen too many Ahabs and Jezebels in the Church. Not in the ho-ish nature that people most associate with Jezebel (although there are some of those in the Church, too). The ho-ish Jezebel is the one mentioned in Revelation, but I am talking about Ahab's wife in First and Second Kings in the Bible. I am talking more of the conniving and manipulative side of Jezebel. I am talking like the pastor isn't even the pastor anymore, just like Ahab ceased to be the king. Jezebel is ruling. She is the puppet master and the puppet reacts at her behest. What does Proverbs 29:2 say? *When the righteous are in authority, the people rejoice: but when the wicked beareth rule, the people mourn.* If there is unrest in the Church and you can't understand why, turn over in the middle of the night, stare your biggest problem in the face, and pray that God reveals how you can solve it. Because no matter how much Ahab may have loved Jezebel, she was his undoing. I'm pretty sure he would like to turn back the clock on her. There are exceptions to the rule. There are pastors who don't really know the Lord (they have just acquired titles throughout the years); they are greedy, they are abusive, and they ho around. Their churches survive because of the godly and sweet spirit of the pastor's wife.

Maybe this has gone unnoticed, but judgment is not coming to the Lord's house—it's already here. There is now a very vivid outward showing of an inward problem that has festered in the Church for years. These pastors and ministers of the Gospel who are walking under the banner of Christianity under false pretenses are going to be dealt with. No longer in secret, these people are having public falls from grace. Why does the congregation have to "wait on the Lord" and "trust God" while the clergy is allowed to lie, cheat, steal, rape, rob, and pillage to get what they want? I learned a lesson a long time ago, and it would be in the best interests of pastors and other ministers of the Gospel if they would learn this lesson and learn it soon. The lesson is that God is not a toy and we are not to play with Him. Remember, class, the lesson will continue until the lesson is learned.

How did we go so far off course? How did we get to the point where we no longer preach the life, death, burial, and resurrection of Christ, but we preach about having faith to get a new house? When did the Church get so gluttonous for money, power, and status that saving and nurturing souls became an afterthought? It's as if we want money and status, and if someone gets saved in the process, that is just gravy. Prosperity may help people down here, but it will not help them make it into heaven.

To the preachers who are preaching prosperity, that's all well and good if people were supposed to strive to make it into the heaven down here, but we should be trying to go to the heaven that the Lord has prepared. This watered-down preaching that has been going on has led to watered-down church folks (remember there is a difference between church folks and Christians). Hell is going to be full of people who thought they could live any kind of way as long as they brought their money to the storehouse. Why do they think that? Because that is what they are being taught. They are being taught that we can buy our way into heaven.

You can't buy your way into heaven! I'm sorry. That is not how we say it now. Buying your way into heaven sounds so bad (it's what people are trying to do, but it doesn't really sound nice).

Let me put it another way. You can't sow your way into heaven! If people could, we would have no need for Jesus. There would be no need for the life, death, burial, and resurrection of Christ. We would all make money and take it to the storehouse, and then we would go to heaven. Please. I am a lot of things, but being foolish is not one of my character traits. *Lay not up for yourselves treasures upon earth, where moth and rust doth corrupt, and where thieves break through and steal: But lay up for yourselves treasures in heaven, where neither moth nor rust doth corrupt, and where thieves do not break through nor steal: For where your treasure is, there will your heart be also* (Matthew 6:19–21). A lot of pastors have their treasure down here on this earth. This is why they have to be more beholden to their congregation than to God. They want what the money can buy, and they have overlooked all God can provide.

The credibility of the Church has been severely damaged. We have forged so many checks in the Lord's name that He almost has no credit down here. Why have we moved holiness and salvation out of the Church? Is it because they are bad for business? Is it because people don't normally put money in the collection plate if they are not told what they want to hear? It is not completely the pastors and ministers of the Gospel's fault, but the majority of this burden does lie square on our shoulders. If we didn't do it, we allowed it to go on, and therefore we are to blame. *Abstain from all appearance of evil* (1 Thessalonians 5:22). We have failed in that area. Now there is very little that the world sees that is good about the Church, because so many pastors and ministers of the Gospel have tainted the Lord's reputation. It has gotten so bad that being good is a reason for skepticism. People see what is going on in the Church, and when a real shepherd or when true Christians come around and want to help and try to do right, they are met with immediate cynicism. There has been so much wrong going on that people don't seem to know how to take it when someone tries to do right. This is sad. Leaders in the Church need to keep themselves according to the standards laid out in the Bible, lest we deter others from the Body. The qualifications of church leaders are in 1 Timothy 3:2–7:

> A bishop then must be blameless, the husband of one wife, vigilant, sober, of good behaviour, given to hospitality, apt to teach;
> Not given to wine, no striker, not greedy of filthy lucre; but patient, not a brawler, not covetous;
> One that ruleth well his own house, having his children in subjection with all gravity;
> (For if a man know not how to rule his own house, how shall he take care of the church of God?)
> Not a novice, lest being lifted up with pride he fall into the condemnation of the devil.
> Moreover he must have a good report of them which are without; lest he fall into reproach and the snare of the devil.

Now I am almost certain that some smart aleck is going to say that this applies just to bishops, but it should apply to all who walk under the banner of Christianity. Verses 2 and 3 seem to be extremely difficult for some to abide by, for some reason. How difficult is it to walk upright before the Lord, not to ho around on your wife, be sober, be watchful, and not covet? Is it really that difficult to be a decent human being?

Verses 4 and 5 are often misconstrued. They are not to be interpreted as ruling a house with an iron fist so that your family is scared of you. There does have to be some rule over the house. Not abuse. There is a fine line, and for whatever reason some people don't know how to have a balance. They go from one extreme to the other and have no middle ground.

Verse 6 says, "Not a novice." Just because someone has been in the church building all of their life does not mean that they are not still a novice. I have seen people draped with titles who couldn't expound on a Scripture if their life depended on it. I have also seen people new to the Lord exalted. I don't doubt that these people have good testimonies and that the testimonies should be shared, but having a good testimony does not mean that that person should be placed over others to teach them the things of God. How is that that people are given titles and positions to lead and cannot convey the Word in which we are to believe?

In verse 7, having a good reputation with those who "are without" means having a good reputation in and out of the Church. This does not mean that the pastors need to be in the club contributing to the local economy by paying the cover charge and indulging in the two-drink minimum, so that they can "fit in." It means that we are not to be purposefully bipolar. We are to be the same in and out of the church building.

Seasons change, but God does not; He is the same yesterday, today, and forevermore. Just because the world changes with the changing times does not mean that the Church is to follow suit. *God is not a man, that he should lie; neither the son of man, that he should repent: hath he said, and shall he not do it? or hath he spoken, and shall he not make it good?* (Numbers 23:19). Everything that He said that He is going to do is going to come to pass. So when God says that if you can't receive correction He will disown you, He means it. Hebrews 12:5–11 bears repeating:

And ye have forgotten the exhortation which speaketh unto
you as unto children, My son, despise not thou the chasten-
ing of the Lord, nor faint when thou art rebuked of him:
For whom the Lord loveth he chasteneth, and scourgeth
every son whom he receiveth.
If ye endure chastening, God dealeth with you as with
sons; for what son is he whom the father chasteneth not?
But if ye be without chastisement, whereof all are partak-
ers, then are ye bastards, and not sons.
Furthermore we have had fathers of our flesh which cor-
rected us, and we gave them reverence: shall we not much
rather be in subjection unto the Father of spirits, and live?
For they verily for a few days chastened us after their own
pleasure; but he for our profit, that we might be partakers
of his holiness.
Now no chastening for the present seemeth to be joyous, but
grievous: nevertheless afterward it yieldeth the peaceable
fruit of righteousness unto them which are exercised thereby.

Don't run to God on Judgment Day calling Him Father,
because for some of these pastors and ministers of the Gospel,
God disowned them a long time ago. I am amazed at what
a title and a position will do to people's minds. They start
thinking that nobody can talk to them, and nobody can correct them. Think again. If by some "Christmas miracle" they
receive correction, they will receive it only from someone of
equal or greater title and position than them. I was not aware
that God spoke only to people with titles. Are we back in the
Old Testament, where I have to go to the priests, so that they

can go to God, so that I may be cleansed of my sins as well? Can the people not go to God for themselves anymore? Since we can talk directly to God now, surely He can talk directly to us without a three-way phone call with our respective pastors. So why do some pastors and ministers of the Gospel think that God will send correction for them only through someone of equal or greater status? It is with people like that that God will eventually have to put their deliverance in the mouth of a donkey (Numbers 22:20–35) just to see if they will humble themselves and receive it.

Where is God in the Church? Just because the temperature rises in the sanctuary does not mean that God is there. It just means that there are a lot of people giving off body heat. It isn't that difficult to follow the Lord. Why do we make things much more difficult than they actually have to be? The Lord is a good master. He lets us know what we do well, and He informs us when we are doing wrong.

Unto the angel of the church of Ephesus write; These things saith he that holdeth the seven stars in his right hand, who walketh in the midst of the seven golden candlesticks;
I know thy works, and thy labour, and thy patience, and how thou canst not bear them which are evil: and thou hast tried them which say they are apostles, and are not, and hast found them liars:
And hast borne, and hast patience, and for my name's sake hast laboured, and hast not fainted.
Nevertheless I have somewhat against thee, because thou hast left thy first love.
Remember therefore from whence thou art fallen, and repent, and do the first works; or else I will come unto thee

*quickly, and will remove thy candlestick out of his place,
except thou repent.*

Revelation 2:1–5

Some of us may be doing everything that we think that we
should be doing, but if we keep reading the Bible, the Word of
God lets us know that there may be some areas where we are still
in lack. We might be doing all of the good things and none of
the bad things, but have we left God, our first love? If so, we need
to run back to Him. Some people get so caught up in doing the
works that they forget why they do the works. They forget God.
If we do nothing else, we need not forget God, and we need to
never leave His side.

*Now the Spirit speaketh expressly, that in the latter times some shall
depart from the faith, giving heed to seducing spirits, and doctrines of devils; Speaking lies in hypocrisy; having their conscience seared with a hot
iron* (1 Timothy 4:1–2). We should all take a look at ourselves and
ask the question, "Is anyone departing from the faith because of our
actions?" Isn't it sad when people flock to the church when a guest
speaker comes in town to do a conference or something? Shouldn't
that tell the pastors that they are not doing their due diligence,
and that their flock is not getting what it needs on a regular basis,
so the flock has to wait until another church imports holiness,
because that is the only way that most of them are going to hear it
preached? They say that most doctors have a "God complex." They
seem to think that life and death are in their hands. Well, if that
is the case, then most pastors have a "David complex." They think
that they can sleep with Bathsheba, kill Uriah, and still be a "man
after God's own heart." Think again. David was not a man after
God's own heart because he sinned; he was a man after God's own

heart because he humbled himself and received correction. Sinners can learn the Bible and convey it well if they are educated. What distinguishes you from them?

> *Take heed therefore unto yourselves, and to all the flock,*
> *over the which the Holy Ghost hath made you overseers, to*
> *feed the church of God, which he hath purchased with his*
> *own blood.*
> *For I know this, that after my departing shall grievous*
> *wolves enter in among you, not sparing the flock.*
> *Also of your own selves shall men arise, speaking perverse*
> *things, to draw away disciples after them.*
>
> Acts 20:28–30

We are commanded to feed the Lord's flock. Why then do we give them milk instead of meat? Why do we water down their juice? Why is it more important to be loved of men than loved of God? These pastors and ministers of the Gospel are drawing away disciples after them. They are building an army for themselves instead of an army for Christ. Have you ever seen people who will defend their pastor and church to the death, but they will not utter a word for the Lord? Whoever they are defending is either a false prophet, a deceiver, or too foolish to know what they are doing to the Lord's flock. Either way they will have to answer for their actions on Judgment Day.

Pastors are doing their flock a great disservice when they do not correct them because they have money, or because they are friends. These people are being loved straight to hell. Correction is withheld, and not only are we loving that person straight to hell, but it also applies to whomever they contaminate in the process. The Bible says in 1 Thessalonians 5:14, *Now we exhort you, brethren, warn them that are unruly, comfort the feebleminded, support the weak, be patient toward all men.* It does not say everybody but your friends are to be warned and corrected.

There are exceptions to the rule. After everything that I have said concerning the pastors and ministers of the Gospel, there are still some out there who are doing the right thing. They are not using people like toilet paper and discarding them. They are not misusing church funds for personal gain. There are some good leaders out there. The only problem is that finding one of those pastors is like trying to find a particular needle in a bucket of needles. The exceptions need to go back to being the norm, and these false teachers and false prophets need to be shown the door.

> *Better is a little with righteousness than great revenues without right.*
>
> Proverbs 16:8

To Myself —

Be Angry and Sin Not

Be ye angry, and sin not: let not the sun go down upon your wrath: Neither give place to the devil

(Ephesians 4:26–27).

Anger. I think that covers it. I am angry about how the Church has mutated. I am angry because these pastors would rather be celebrities than shepherds. I am angry that these pastors want for nothing while some in the congregation can barely support their families. In the midst of my anger, I am trying to fight off bitterness with all that I have, but I may be losing that battle.

So, I think that it is pretty safe to say that I didn't follow Ephesians 4:26 to a T. I have allowed the sun to go down on my anger many a time. I have, however, managed to keep the devil at bay—for now. I can't say with all honesty that I won't allow him to seep in if I see another clergyman's sins overlooked because of their position and their monetary earning potential, or if I hear about another unnecessary building fund or "our millionaire leader lost his car and the church needs to replace it for him" fund. Really? As if the Church didn't buy it for him in the first place. I'm pretty sure the other five cars that he has are pleased because now he can drive them instead of letting them sit in his garage. Well, there I go letting the devil seep in.

Don't get me wrong, I don't fly off the handle at the blink of an eye. I take a lot of crap, and I take it for a long period of time, but after a few months or a year or two, enough is enough. When I get to my boiling point, the fruits of the spirit start to fly out of the window, and it is best for me to separate myself, lest I tell these perpetrating "Christians" how I feel about them.

But the fruit of the Spirit is love, joy, peace, longsuffering, gentleness, goodness, faith,
Meekness, temperance: against such there is no law.
And they that are Christ's have crucified the flesh with the affections and lusts.
If we live in the Spirit, let us also walk in the Spirit.
Let us not be desirous of vain glory, provoking one another, envying one another.

Galatians 5:22–26

I'm not going to lie. Bitterness is trying to fight its way in, and, I may not have the strength or desire to stop fighting it off. At times it feels like anger and bitterness are tag teaming on me. The emotions sometimes appear to take turns. When bitterness reared its head and subsided, my anger was right there to take its place. It's like a person whose rash goes away, and within minutes his hemorrhoids flare up.

I allowed my anger to justify allowing a little bitterness in at times, but I was wrong. I was mad. It took the Lord a while to restore my love and forgiveness of people. I didn't have any stomach for foolishness. My foolishness tolerance level is currently at "extremely low" and quickly falling to "nonexistent" as far as foolishness in the Body of Christ is concerned. Here is the rule of thumb for people who bring foolishness around me: if someone brings foolishness to me, there is a high probability that that individual will leave with the foolishness that they came with. Depending on my response, they are going to leave with a little less self-esteem than they came in with as well (the Lord is working on gentleness with me, too).

Let me give an example of some of the foolishness in the Body. In the Church, the bigger the sinner, the quicker they climb up the corporate ladder in the Church. Saved folks don't matter. They are an obstacle and they are in the way—a speed bump on the drive to the bank. Isn't that right? Forgive my anger (or ignorance of the matter; somebody help me out here), but I was under the impression that we were not supposed to conform to this world. But the Church is conforming and complying at an alarming rate.

I may have been a little subtle, so it is quite possible that some have not noticed my high level of contempt for people who go into the ministry for the primary purpose of making money. I am sick of these money-grubbing whores in the Church passing themselves off as pastors and ministers of the Gospel. I honestly believe that there is a special place in hell for whoever came up with the $100-line crap. I cannot begin to count how many people that single act of greed has deterred from the Body. Is anointing and salvation worth so little now that we are willing to sell it to the highest bidder? The next thing that I know, people are going to be selling prime real estate in heaven at the right hand of the Father on the Internet. The sad thing is some moron would actually try to purchase it. I mean, isn't that what we are doing now? Are we not selling blessings, selling favor, selling salvation?

It's free! Jesus already paid the price, so how dare these greedy ingrates try to repackage and sell it?

Could someone clarify something for me? Since for the last few years we have been selling everything under the sun, does that mean that the missionaries in these third-world countries need to come back home? Does that mean that there is no need for the Church to waste its time with people who cannot afford to buy a blessing? Does that mean that if people all over the world don't have a certain income, that God does not love them? Is this what we are telling people? Is this the crap that is being spread now? These pastors and ministers of the Gospel may not be saying it quite like that, but that is the message that is being sent: if you have a good job, money in the bank, big house, three or four cars, and other tangible wealth, then God loves you. I mean, isn't that what we are telling people? That if God loves you or favors you, you ought to be able to "show some sign" of that through tangible wealth? Whatever happened to the fact that I was not purchased with corruptible things such as silver and gold, but I was bought with the blood of the lamb (1 Peter 1:18–19)?

Church services have ceased to be a time of worship and have turned into social hour. *And I will give you pastors according to mine heart, which shall feed you with knowledge and understanding* (Jeremiah 3:15). Well, where is the knowledge and understanding? Pastors don't need knowledge, they have the Internet. They don't need understanding, they have other people in the church for that. Pastors are hype men for the deacons getting ready to take offering. I would like to ask something of the pastors and ministers of the Gospel. Please stop preaching to get me high for the moment and make sure that I put a little extra in the collection plate, but preach the Word so that I have something to hold on to during my daily walk with Christ on this earth.

I don't like these cliques in the Church. People think that everyone wants to be a part of their cliques because they are the "most popular" or have the most titles, but I desire to be a part of nobody's group just to say that I belong. I have seen some people in the Church sell their souls so the pastor, the pastor's wife, and their entourage will throw them an extra nod and wink every once in a while. The devil is a liar, and so are you if you think that I am going to give up my place in the Kingdom for an extra nod and wink.

There was a time that I used to feel like Jeremiah. A lot of people immediately jump to, "Jeremiah said it's like fire shut up in my bones." Yes, eventually he did express that, but before he made that statement he was in a much different state of mind.

> *For since I spake, I cried out, I cried violence and spoil;*
> *because the word of the LORD was made a reproach unto*
> *me, and a derision, daily.*
> *Then I said, I will not make mention of him, nor speak*
> *any more in his name. But his word was in mine heart as*
> *a burning fire shut up in my bones, and I was weary with*
> *forbearing, and I could not stay.*
>
> Jeremiah 20:8–9

Jeremiah told the Lord that he was done. He told the Lord that he wouldn't even speak His name anymore. But Jeremiah's anger was like mine—short-lived. The love of God was so strong that it was as if a fire was burning inside (remember, "God don't need no matches, He's fire all by himself").

There was also a long time when I felt like the Bible describes Jerusalem in Ezekiel 13:16—I thought that I would know no peace. At some point, and I forget when, I went on auto-pilot and began to get even more frustrated. I was frustrated with the people all around me who were playing church so much that they didn't even recognize that I was dying right in the midst of them. I was almost dead on the inside, and no one noticed, and no one cared. I even tried to share it with some people. They either scattered from me like cockroaches in the light, or they tried to avoid me and herd me along like I was nothing more than cattle.

How is it that we are expected to continue to produce in the church like a milked cow, but no one is concerned about our well-being? I guess no one cares if a part of the machine is broken as long as the machine still produces. I learned my lesson with that. I don't think that I will ever share with anyone how I am truly feeling anymore. What would be the point? The reactions that I received from trying to talk to people were at times more painful than what I was going through. I have resolved within myself that I will go back to what I used to do; I will suffer in silence. It is much less painful that way.

Why is my soul not more valuable to you than money, sex, power, or whatever it is that you are seeking when you walk in that church building? If you stop and think about it, these leaders can get more money, they can have more sex, and they can even gain more power, but I have only one soul. Once I am gone and my soul is lost, there is no hope for me. I can't get that back. Why can't anyone see that? Why do I constantly have to feel like I am fighting in a battle that most of the soldiers left a long time ago? Why do I care about people's souls, and they clearly don't? If they do care, they have been beaten for so long that they have finally submitted.

That "Army of One" thing doesn't work so well when you are supposed to be in the Army of the Lord. We are supposed to fight together. Where are my sisters and brothers in Christ who will stand up and say enough is enough? Where are the ones who say we are not going to build another sanctuary, but we are going to use that money to teach the Word of God, and truly help people? Where are the people who don't strive to get the next title and position, but they strive to make sure that others are taken care of and receiving the Word? Where are my brothers and sisters in Christ who will change the measuring stick in the Body? Where are the ones who will stand with me and say that we are not going to count butts in seats, but we are going to nurture souls?

Somebody, anybody, stand with me. Enough is enough. It irritates me to stay silent and let things continue to go on for the sake of not rocking the boat. Maybe that is the problem. People have become so complacent that the boat isn't moving, and it is in stagnant waters. We have caused some permanent damage to the Body. There are some souls that have been lost forever because of our foolishness. Please believe we will answer for that on the Day of Judgment. We will answer for all of this foolishness and wickedness that we have participated in and turned a blind eye to. We can't do anything about those who are already lost, but we can repent and get it right from now on.

I was raised. I wasn't half raised, and I wasn't neglected. My mother did her job with me. One of the best compliments that I have ever received was someone telling me that I was just like my mother. I love that compliment, but I can never be my mother. I truly believe if she stays her course until the Lord calls her home, she will have a crown in heaven. But I can't ride my mother's coattails to heaven. I can't live a life that is displeasing to God and think that when I stand before Him He will let me in because of who my mom is. I have to know the Lord for myself.

If the Lord sees fit to call my mother home, and she doesn't leave me a dime, I have already received my inheritance. She has instilled in me the things of God from an early age. She has shown me how to walk upright before the Lord in teaching and by example. Woe unto me if I let the cares of this world cause me to squander my inheritance. I remember as a child my mother telling me that I was not raised up for the swine. She let me know early on that I was God's child, and I was to conduct myself as such. My mother isn't the most educated woman in the world, but I shudder to think of where I and my relationship with God would be if she had focused more on education than on holiness. Life and the Lord have taught my mother some things that money can't buy and a textbook can't teach. One of the reasons that I love her so much is that she taught me those lessons so that I would not fall by the wayside unnecessarily. When I describe my relationship with my mother, I normally tell people that we are like Elijah and Elisha, and I am trying to get my double portion (2 Kings 2:9). My mother is saved and I am saved, but salvation is not a hereditary trait. The anointing is not hereditary, but it is transferrable. We are not like Eli and his sons. My mother is my mother and my friend, but I will receive swift rebuke from her if I get out of the will of God.

I have been called a hard taskmaster, and I have been called the Angel of Death. I would have to concede on both. Let me explain something about myself. The first book of the Bible that I read was not Genesis, it was not the Gospels, it was Revelation. I don't have an "in the beginning" mentality from reading Genesis, although I believe and I am well aware that everything stemmed from God. I don't have a "grace and mercy" mentality from reading the Gospels, but I do know that I am saved by grace (Ephesians 2:8), the Lord is full of grace and truth (John1:14), and that

I need God's mercy (Matthew 5:7). I also know that there is going to come a time when my Lord ceases to be my Savior and commences to be my judge. From reading the book of Revelation, I have a "get it right or go to hell" mentality. Tomorrow and, more than likely, today is going to be Judgment Day for someone, so there is no time to mess around. So, yes, I am a hard taskmaster, because my mind-set is a product of the Book of Revelation. If something is wrong with that, then I don't know what to tell you. As far as being called the Angel of Death, I won't lie, it did hurt my feelings a little bit, but I had to be reminded that just like the Lord sent Gabriel and Michael, He unleashed the angel of death as well (the Bible refers to him at times as the destroyer).

Proverbs 15:1 says, *A soft answer turneth away wrath: but grievous words stir up anger.* Lord knows that I am working on my delivery, but some stuff you have to come out and say it the way it is and don't beat around the bush. Stop sugarcoating this crap. It's still crap. You can put lipstick on a pig, but at the end of the day it is still as pig and not a woman. Call a spirit a spirit instead of making excuses for it. I have begged the Lord to remove some of the things that I see, hear, and feel. I guess the old saying is right—ignorance is bliss. I was perfectly happy going to church and not seeing the winking, nodding, compromising, and everything else. God has not removed it, but writing my frustrations down has helped alleviate some of the physical pain and spiritual heaviness. I guess my sensitivity to the things that plague the body of Christ is the thorn in my flesh. As with Paul, it will remain with me always, but I can hold on to the fact that God's grace is sufficient (2 Corinthians 12:7–9).

The Church is now like a family that doesn't have enough turkey for Thanksgiving, and they try to offset the lack of meat with side dishes. The meat of the Word has disappeared from the

Church tables so much that churches are scrambling to fill the void with a plethora of alternatives (e.g., the singles ministry, the "soon to be single" ministry, the "I'm married but I want to be single" ministry, the young people ministry, the old people ministry, the "I have some free time on Tuesday night" ministry). But just as the natural body requires water and sustenance to function properly, the Body of Christ also requires the bread of life, the living water, and the meat of the Word. It is as if churches are trying to overcompensate for there being no meat at the table, so they are serving unnecessary and often unfulfilling side dishes. And my soul grieves.

I feel like I am in a very bad position.

And Paul, earnestly beholding the council, said, Men and brethren, I have lived in all good conscience before God until this day.
And the high priest Ananias commanded them that stood by him to smite him on the mouth.
Then said Paul unto him, God shall smite thee, thou whited wall: for sittest thou to judge me after the law, and commandest me to be smitten contrary to the law?
And they that stood by said, Revilest thou God's high priest?
Then said Paul, I wist not, brethren, that he was the high priest: for it is written, Thou shalt not speak evil of the ruler of thy people.

Acts 23:1–5

In Acts 23:3, Paul talks back to a high priest. He does this because the priest has broken the law that he was supposed to uphold. When the bystanders see this in verse 4, they ask *Revilest thou God's high priest?* Paul's response is how I feel. Paul says that he wishes the man that he had to talk back to was not a high priest. That is how I feel.

Why are the voices of correction being drowned out in the Body? Why have we lifted up these pastors and ministers of the Gospel over Christ and deemed their words and deeds to be justified, even when they are not? I wish others would stand with me. Why are there so few people who are willing to call out the "high priests"? I think that my life would be a lot easier if most of the problems in the Body didn't stem from the head and work themselves down. No one says too much when you chastise a lay member, but chastising the clergy in the pulpit will make you have to run for your life. But someone has to say something—all of this stuff has been allowed to go on far too long.

I have learned that when someone believes that they can do no wrong, they have no incentive to do right. No one ever says anything to pastors and the ministers of the Gospel, and I guess that is where the David or God complex comes in. Pastors and ministers feel infallible because no one holds them responsible for their actions. We have allowed them to think that even when they are wrong, they are right. I have heard people actually say, if you don't agree with the pastor, then just leave. What does leaving accomplish? The pastors will continue doing what they are doing without a sounding board, without someone giving godly counsel. *Blessed is the man that walketh not in the counsel of the ungodly, nor standeth in the way of sinners, nor sitteth in the seat of the scornful* (Psalm 1:1). Oh, these pastors are receiving counsel, but most times it is not from the saved and sanctified. Most of the time it is from those who are "helping" bring in more revenue. To receive no Godly counsel is almost no different than dictatorship. The Church is not supposed to be a dictatorship. Pastors are not all-knowing, but the more we treat them that way, the more they will believe it. Yes, God placed pastors over houses, but He did so with the intention of the pastors following His guidance, and not their own.

A lot of people repent in private and rebuke in public. I don't want to be like that. So to go along with my public scathing rebuke of the Body of Christ, here is my public repentance. I do not want to be like this anymore. I'm tired of the rat race and the roller coasters. There was a time when I allowed my anger to consume me, and I was wrong for that. But no more. Either the Church will get it right, or the real saved folks are going to get off the ride. Don't get me wrong now. I don't mean that we are going to walk away from the Lord, but we will walk away from the foolishness in the church building. We are not going to go against the Scripture either. We are not going to forsake the assembly of ourselves, but we are not going to assemble with foolishness.

> *For the time is come that judgment must begin at the house of God: and if it first begin at us, what shall the end be of them that obey not the gospel of God?*
> *And if the righteous scarcely be saved, where shall the ungodly and the sinner appear?*
> *Wherefore let them that suffer according to the will of God commit the keeping of their souls to him in well doing, as unto a faithful Creator.*
>
> 1 Peter 4:17–19

My heart bleeds for people, because 1 Peter 4:18 says that the believers are going to scarcely make it in. So, what about the souls that are going to be lost while the believers are fighting one another? The Church has been paying the minimum balance on its debt. We are trying to do the bare minimum to get into heaven, and that is sad. My soul longs for the day when Church will be Church again. Even if it doesn't happen in this life, I will learn to be content in waiting for it in the next. The sad truth is church isn't church anymore, and it will never be the same. I love the Lord. I love the Church. Thinking about the fact that holiness and salvation are no longer welcome in the Church is a hard pill to swallow for me, and I am having trouble finding enough water to try to get it down. The fact is, church will never be the way it was again, and chances are it is just going to get worse from here. If the Church does not go back to holiness and salvation, instead of meeting each other in heaven, there will be some reunions in hell.

So where do I fall? I have shown no regard for titles or positions. I have exposed from the pulpit to the door. What does that make me? Am I now a backbiter? Should I have invoked my Miranda rights and remained silent? Am I disobedient and out of line? Honestly, I don't know the answer to that. But either way, I think that I would have been more out of line if I would have said nothing and allowed all of this to continue.

Looking diligently lest any man fail of the grace of God; lest any root of bitterness springing up trouble you, and thereby many be defiled (Hebrews 12:15). There was a time when bitterness set in and defiled me. No more. *For I am persuaded, that neither death, nor life, nor angels, nor principalities, nor powers, nor things present, nor things to come, Nor height, nor depth, nor any other creature, shall be able to separate us from the love of God, which is in Christ Jesus our Lord* (Romans 8:38–39). So much is going on that I often pray and cry out to the Lord, "Lord, don't forget about me." But even if I don't get the things that I want in this life, I will continue on with my Lord. The Lord is not a casual acquaintance to me; we have a real relationship. My soul is too valuable to me! If that means that for the rest of my life I will be on the outside looking in, then so be it. If no one else does right, I will stand and do right. I have no other choice. My biggest fear is that I will lead others to Christ and miss Him myself.

> *But I keep under my body, and bring it into subjection: lest that by any means, when I have preached to others, I myself should be a castaway.*
>
> 1 Corinthians 9:27

To All

The Lord Is On His Way

We have received ample time to get it right. The Lord is on His way back, and we have the Churches in Revelation still prominent in today's world. We have the Church of Ephesus, which was the loveless church; the Church of Smyrna, which was the persecuted church; the Church of Pergamos, which was the church that was too lenient; the Church of Thyatira, which was the compromising church; the Church of Sardis, which was the lifeless church; the Church of Philadelphia, which was the obedient church; and the Church of the Laodiceans, which was the lukewarm church. Of the seven churches, the one that is the least prominent is the obedient church like the one in Philadelphia.

We have tried to get God to conform to us, instead of the other way around. The Lord will crack the sky again, and we will have our eternal judgment. So we better get right!

And the times of this ignorance God winked at; but now commandeth all men every where to repent:
Because he hath appointed a day, in the which he will judge the world in righteousness by that man whom he

149

hath ordained; whereof he hath given assurance unto all
men, in that he hath raised him from the dead.

Acts 17:30–31

God is not going to "wink" at this stuff any longer. God
will not allow the sinners and those who overlooked the sin to get
away with this any longer. He is not going to allow someone who
is partially clean to make it into heaven.

Stop trying to create and be comfortable in a heaven down
here. Maybe one of the problems is that people have been describ-
ing heaven too much. I have always said that I wish people would
talk about hell more. Some people actually think that hell is
going to be one big party where they will drink, smoke, have sex,
and party at their leisure. I have always thought if people gave an
accurate description of hell, we would want to go to heaven even
if it was a shack near the ocean during hurricane season.

I saw a man named Bill Wiese on a show one Sunday morning being interviewed by Jentezen Franklin. Mr. Wiese began to
discuss how God had allowed him to spend twenty-three minutes
in hell to see what it was like. He described hell in such a way
that I had never heard before. He talked about the constant tor-
ture and the complete absence of God. The same way we have a
misguided view of the crucifixion because of the picture of Jesus
that we have on our walls with the one drop of blood, we have
no true depiction of hell. When Mr. Wiese summed up his inter-
view, he said that people put "great effort into a short holiday and
no effort into eternity." That is so true. *The wicked shall be turned*
into hell, and all the nations that forget God (Psalm 9:17).

There are those that criticize Christians for being narrow-
minded, and we should be narrow-minded. *Enter ye in at the strait*

gate: for wide is the gate, and broad is the way, that leadeth to destruction, and many there be which go in thereat: Because strait is the gate, and narrow is the way, which leadeth unto life, and few there be that find it (Matthew 7:13–14). Narrow is the way, and we don't want to go down Broad Street. Broad Street is how all of this stuff that is contrary to the Word of God has been allowed to rear its ugly head in the Body.

I often sit back and think, what if the Lord were to do to the Body of Christ what He did in Egypt in Moses' time? What if God were to unleash the Death Angel on the Body of Christ? How many of us would be covered in the blood and come out unscathed? What if God gave specific instructions of going through the Body and removing the perpetrators, those who are doing wrong, and all kinds of atrocities in the Lord's name, under the banner of Christianity? What would happen if Christ purged His body? What if the Lord had the Death Angel do a body scan over the Body of Christ and purge it of its diseases? One day we are going to realize that God is not a toy, and we are not to play with Him.

No matter who we are, we as humans have an unmatched ability to justify our sins. But the Bible says in Isaiah 5:20, *Woe unto them that call evil good, and good evil; that put darkness for light, and light for darkness; that put bitter for sweet, and sweet for bitter!* Remember, people will stay in their sin as long as no one says anything about it. If we wonder how people cannot believe in Christ and how our loved ones can grow up around the Church and still be half-hearted fakers and sometimes not even be Christians at all, we need only look in the mirror at the pathetic example that we are providing them. Sometimes people say that we are the only Bible that people will ever read, but some of us are not a representation of the Word. There are some trashy novels and bindings with blank pages trying to pass themselves off as a walking representation of the Word. We will be held accountable for all of this on the Day of Judgment. In that hour, we will not be able to point fingers and pass blame. We cannot blame someone else for our own personal shortcomings. The perpetrators against us will have to give an account for that, but we have to take responsibility for how we respond to others' actions.

The Bible is the wonderful Word of God. I would love for everyone to read it. Read your Bibles; there is nothing going on in this world that has not happened in the Bible or that the Bible has not foretold. Before trying to interpret it, find out the initial context in which it was written. So many times things are lost in translation, and what is trying to be conveyed is overlooked. Read the Bible and love our Lord and Savior. I learn something new as I continue to read through the Bible, study, and grow in God. Please look inside and ask God to help make changes where changes need to be made. Because when the Lord cracks the sky, the time of preparation is over. He expects us to be ready when He calls. The Bible is the Word of God. I have quoted numerous passages to encourage the reading of the Word, and to show that it is applicable during our daily walk with Christ.

> *Now this I say, brethren, that flesh and blood cannot inherit the kingdom of God; neither doth corruption inherit incorruption.*
> *Behold, I shew you a mystery; We shall not all sleep, but we shall all be changed,*
> *In a moment, in the twinkling of an eye, at the last trump: for the trumpet shall sound, and the dead shall be raised incorruptible, and we shall be changed.*

For this corruptible must put on incorruption, and this
mortal must put on immortality.
So when this corruptible shall have put on incorruption,
and this mortal shall have put on immortality, then shall
be brought to pass the saying that is written, Death is
swallowed up in victory.
O death, where is thy sting? O grave, where is thy victory?
The sting of death is sin; and the strength of sin is the law.
But thanks be to God, which giveth us the victory through
our Lord Jesus Christ.
Therefore, my beloved brethren, be ye stedfast, unmoveable,
always abounding in the work of the Lord, forasmuch as ye
know that your labour is not in vain in the Lord.

1 Corinthians 15:50–58

1 Corinthians 15:52 says He is coming in the twinkling of
an eye. The Bride is to be ready at all times, because the Bridegroom can start the wedding ceremony at any time. No man
knows the day nor the hour when the Lord shall arrive (Matthew
24:36 and Mark 13:32).

Forasmuch as ye know that ye were not redeemed with cor-
ruptible things, as silver and gold, from your vain conver-
sation received by tradition from your fathers;
But with the precious blood of Christ, as of a lamb without
blemish and without spot:

1 Peter 1:18–19

THE BENEDICTION—

It's Done!

I believe that the Chicago Mass Choir said it best: "I Pray We'll All Be Ready for His Return." This book may be offensive to some. I will take that. I will be the lightning rod for the offense. Because I would rather offend people now than for God to offend them when He says, "Depart from me" (Matthew 7:23). If I offend, then there will be time to get right, but after the Lord's offense, eternity is sealed. There will be no do-overs.

There is some truth to the critics' allegations, and we must begin to try to make things right. What can wash away my sin? What can make me whole again? Nothing but the blood of Jesus.** I have pointed out a lot of the bad, because people keep overlooking it and sweeping things under the rug, but there are some people out there (and some of them are even pastors and ministers of the Gospel) who are determined to do right and stand for God no matter what the cost. For those people, I have nothing but respect, because it is hard swimming against the current of a corrupt ocean.

The purpose of writing this book was not to offend, but we have to get things right. Until the problems in the Church are laid

---

** "Nothing but the Blood of Jesus."

out, they cannot be dealt with. We have to stop covering up what is going on, but bring it to light and fix it. When the Lord cracks the sky, we have to be one hundred percent ready because ninety-nine and a half won't do.[††] My prayer is that we are all heaven ready when the Lord calls.

Much Love,

Tiffany

For the wages of sin is death; but the gift of God is eternal life through Jesus Christ our Lord.

Romans 6:23

[††]   "Ninety-nine and a Half," old devotional song

www.ingramcontent.com/pod-product-compliance
Lightning Source LLC
LaVergne TN
LVHW092323080426
835508LV00039B/514